RESCUING RILEY, SAVING MYSELF

RESCUING RILEY, SAVING MYSELF

A Man and His Dog's Struggle to Find Salvation

Zachary Anderegg

with Pete Nelson

Skyhorse Publishing

Skyhorse Publishing books may be purchased in bulk at special discounts for
sales promotion, corporate gifts, fund-raising, or educational purposes. Special
editions can also be created to specifications. For details, contact the Special Sales
Department, Skyhorse Publishing, 307 West 36th Street, 11th Floor, New York,
NY 10018 or info@skyhorsepublishing.com.

Skyhorse® and Skyhorse Publishing® are registered trademarks of Skyhorse
Publishing, Inc.®, a Delaware corporation.

www.skyhorsepublishing.com

10 9 8 7 6 5 4 3 2 1

Library of Congress Cataloging-in-Publication Data

Anderegg, Zak.
    Rescuing Riley, saving myself : a man and his dog's struggle to find salvation /
Zak Anderegg with Pete Nelson.
        pages cm
    Hardcover ISBN 978-1-62636-170-6 (alkaline paper) 1. Anderegg, Zak.
2. Dog owners--United States--Biography. 3. Dogs--United States--Biography.
4. Dog rescue--Arizona. 5. Dog rescue--Psychological aspects. 6. Salvation.
7. Human-animal relationships--United States. 8. Anderegg, Zak--Childhood
and youth. 9. Abused children--United States--Biography. 10. Bullying--
Psychological aspects--United States. I. Nelson, Pete, 1953- II. Title.
    SF422.82.A63A3 2013
    636.0092--dc23
    [B]
                                                        2013032922
Paperback ISBN: 978-1-63450-218-4
Ebook ISBN: 978-1-62873-530-7

Cover design by Mary Belibasakis

Printed in the United States of America

ACKNOWLEDGMENTS

The names of people who have played a part in this story are simply too numerous to account for. Some people have been directly involved in helping transform this story into a tangible piece of work while others played a crucial role in my past, knowingly or not, giving me life experiences for better or worse that would one day culminate in the total telling of my story.

Certain people stand out as being particularly significant throughout this process. I can only hope that those whose names inevitably fail to receive mention realize that their roles in my life were nevertheless critical in creating the life experiences shared in this book.

Pete S.

Had you not approached me that day up in the weight room, I know in my heart my life would not have been altered for the better, at least not then. Your devotion as a workout partner and decency as a human being are appreciated more than I will ever be able to express. You didn't just show me how to get my body in shape back then; you helped put me on a track that forever changed who I would become. You may very well have saved my life! I am forever grateful to you.

Cheryl M.

You filled a void in my life when I dearly needed someone I could trust. You withheld judgment and treated me like one of your own. I tried to tell you back then how much that meant to me. I hope you never question the role you've played in my life and how much I value our "kitchen table talks" and the times I shared with your family.

Page Animal Hospital staff
I have the utmost respect and gratitude for each and every one of you who played a role in helping me save Riley's life. From the kind woman who provided me with a cat carrier after hours on Sunday evening to the technicians and doctors who saved my dog's life, I thank you all! You are special people doing very special work.

Mary M.
You were there, like you always are, when I needed your help. I needed to regroup after dealing with the darkness that surrounded Riley and you didn't even hesitate when I asked for your help. In those days spent healing, Riley came to trust you. He surely saw the same kind heart and gentle spirit in you that Michelle and I do, and I am honored to have you as a friend. Thank you.

Ellen Degeneres
Riley and his brother eat better than Michelle and I do thanks to you! His health could not be better under the circumstances and I know his diet is a huge part of that. Thank you, Ellen, for your generous donation of Halo dog food to my two boys. And thank you for your personal generosity to Michelle and me.

Alli, George, and Elizabeth
Each of you has played a critical role along this path I find myself on. The timing of your entry into my life almost seems planned. And yes, Alli, I know that's what you keep telling me. I could not

have made the progress that I have or posses the self-awareness I have acquired had it not been for each of you. I didn't feel like just a "client." I felt like you truly cared about my well-being and wanted to help me. For that I am forever grateful to each of you!

Carolyn J.
We share a difficult past, that's for sure. I remember thinking, "How could someone just go and write a book about such personal details?" Well, I can now relate. The writing that led to this book began the day after we had dinner together. Your words hit me just the right way. I struggled to see what it was you were telling me, but in retrospect I don't know that you could've been more right on. Thank you so much for your advice and friendship. I wish you the very best going forward and hope you and B have a long and wonderful life together! Hope to see you again soon.

Madeleine M.
Only fate can explain how I got your number through Carolyn. Funny how things happen sometimes. It is not lost on me that had you not read my draft, had you not stuck with me in spite of my impatience, none of this would have happened. I still owe you dinner, and being privy to your finer tastes in life, your Prada habit coming to mind, I can only hope book sales are strong enough to allow me to fulfill my obligation to you. Any chance Wendy's would suffice?

Steve Ross
Here's hoping for a successful project for the two of us.

Pete Nelson
You took my raw material and weaved the story now memorialized in these pages. I hope we are able to touch many lives for the better.

Nicole Frail

It has been a true pleasure working with you, Nicole. From the beginning you have bridged a critical gap between honoring what I want and what is in the best interest of the story. Your consideration and professionalism are both noted and appreciated. You deserve much success and I wish you the best!

Michelle

You have stuck with me through thick and thin. We've always been each other's biggest fans. We walked each other down the aisle at Wind Point. Somehow it just feels like that's where we belong, always next to each other taking life on, together.

This process has been long and difficult. You know that more than anyone. We've come a long way and learned an awful lot, about each other, ourselves, and life itself. Time will tell where we go from here. Had someone told us that my trip south that Saturday morning would lead to a new member of the family and a published book, we would have both laughed. But deep down would we really have been surprised? I don't know, it just seems to be the way our lives go together.

I cannot thank you enough for your love and support throughout everything. You chose me; therefore, you chose a difficult path. I hope the rewards have been satisfying and the memories worth making. I look forward to the future, to our future, side by side, taking on the world as we always do.

CHARACTER—

Doing what's right when nobody is watching.

INTRODUCTION

Had someone told me that my trip to the desert that Saturday morning would result in my writing a book, I wouldn't have believed them. I wouldn't have thought I'd have a story to tell, or that anything would happen worthy of a book. I'd read somewhere that everyone has a book inside them, waiting to be written. *Rescuing Riley, Saving Myself* is mine; it's the story I had to tell. But that Saturday morning, I couldn't have known it.

The idea came to me when many of Riley's fans on Facebook suggested I write something about the rescue. Merely as a dog rescue story, there was some drama to it, but I questioned if there was enough depth for a book. I knew I could write up the technical aspects and tell how I set up my rope system, all the contingencies I had to take into account, and the techniques I improvised to ascend with a dog in tow, but it didn't seem like enough to fill the pages of a book.

It wasn't until I was having dinner one night with friends that it occurred to me: I had more to tell than just a wilderness rescue story. One guest that night was my friend, Carolyn, an accomplished bestselling author who said I needed to write an adult memoir about not only the rescue, but also how it was placed in the larger context of my past. She knew enough about me to know that in that respect, there was something worth telling. The following day, I sat down and wrote fifteen pages. Within ten days, I had written more than 150 pages, and the surprising part was that those pages contained not one, but two stories.

What I didn't know, until I sat down to write, was that writing a book isn't a process where first you think up a book and then you write it down. Rather, you discover the book as you write it. In a way, it's almost like exploring a canyon, where you keep going without knowing what's around the next corner, take each obstacle or technical section as it arrives, come prepared but improvise as you move forward, and, when you reach the end, it somehow all makes sense.

It was a surreal experience. I started typing on my laptop, simply talking about this dog I rescued. The next thing I knew, totally unexpectedly, I found myself digging into my past, as scenes and experiences from my early childhood kept coming forward, begging to be written down. At first it didn't make sense, but as I wrote, I slowly realized how many parallels existed between what happened to Riley and what had happened to me as I was growing up. I never saw it coming; it just happened. Once I understood this connection, a door opened, presenting an opportunity to understand something important about how people can be cruel to animals—and to each other. Riley and I had both faced adversity and cruelty, and I rescued him, but as I reflected on it, he rescued me, too. Coming to this conclusion was . . . indescribable.

As I wrote, I made a promise to myself to be brutally honest about everything I wanted to discuss. This book is an account of my life, something that would stay on the bookshelves—either real bookshelves in brick and mortar buildings or digital "bookshelves" in some computer server somewhere—long after I'm gone, and I wanted to leave behind the truth as best I could tell it. I knew that some of the events I would include would not be flattering to me or show me in the best light. I knew that some topics I would discuss were so deeply personal that even my wife of thirteen years wasn't fully aware of the details.

I chose to tell as much truth as I could because, in the end, as therapeutic and revealing as the writing process has been for me, this book is not for *me*. I had to tell the full truth because I want my readers to really understand the effect abuse has on the abused. Bullying is sometimes dismissed as just a normal part of growing up, something that happens and then everybody outgrows it and moves on, when in fact recent studies have shown it can have a lifelong, permanent deleterious effect on the kids who get bullied. In my experience, in its most extreme forms, bullying is nothing short of pure evil. Until we frame it as such, we will continue to dismiss it as a negative but normal part of the maturation process, nothing more than "growing pains," albeit severe ones, and as long as we dismiss it, kids will continue to suffer. As long as we dismiss it, or underestimate it, the kids who are most traumatized will feel like no one takes them seriously, no one understands, and many of them will, tragically, conclude that the only way to end the anguish is to take their own lives.

This book is not for me. It's for the kids who've been bullied, but it's also for the abusers—the bullies who find it amusing to torture or torment kids and classmates who seem weak or withdrawn or vulnerable and bullies who abuse either emotionally or physically, unaware of the damage they're doing. It's also for the friends of the bullies, or the kids who stand by and witness bullying but say nothing and do nothing about it. I didn't want to write to condemn anyone as much as to raise awareness, but if I could hope to raise awareness in any one group, it would be for the kids who resort to bullying, many of whom probably don't understand why they do it and who certainly give little thought to the consequences of their actions. If my story doesn't resonate with them, perhaps Riley's will.

It was in that regard that I found the strength to dig deeply into myself by once again experiencing events and thoughts I never would have imagined sharing with the world, even if it meant reopening wounds and revisiting hurts that I've been trying my whole life to forget. I've written this book with the hope of changing how we treat each other. I would like to change the way we treat each other on as broad a scale as possible, but if I can change the way one bully treats one victim, or the way one victim sees his own life, and if I can make that one victim see that it's not always going to be so hard, then I will be satisfied.

What I didn't expect was that by writing a book in the grand hope of changing the world, or the smaller hope of changing my readers, I too would be transformed. I have come to see myself, and my relationship with the world, and my relationship with my family, in a new way. A better, more balanced way. I have gone back deep into the dark canyon of myself, and I've climbed out, intact and improved.

To a great extent, I have Riley to thank for that. I am in no way grateful that he had to suffer the way he did, but I am thankful that I could help save him and for the lessons he's taught me. When I think of what he went through, and how he came out the other side better for it, it gives me hope. I've wondered what would happen if Riley ever met the person who hurt him, but I don't really think he would hold a grudge. What I see in him, every day, is how overwhelmed with gratitude he is for the life he has and how he refuses to let his prior suffering deform him or dim his dogged optimism. He doesn't carry his pain with him, and so he seems to have healed without any scars. We humans have larger brains and better memories than dogs do, but sometimes that means we don't let go of things the way we should—the way Riley has. Before I found Riley, there were so many things I could not let go of, but now . . .

But now it's all in the book, and now that it is, I don't have to carry it around inside me. I don't have to carry it at all. I can live like Riley does, tail wagging, full speed ahead and moving forward, not backward. I don't believe in fate, or think, as some people do, that everything happens for a reason. Practically speaking, ninety-nine out of one hundred things happen for no reason at all, but this book is about that one time, one day on the Colorado Plateau, when I walked into a canyon, and my life was forever changed.

I would like to warn the reader to be prepared. What you are about to read is uncensored. Parts of it will be raw and unflinching and might make you feel uncomfortable. My intention is to tell my story as I remember it. And, as my wife Michelle can attest, when recalling how I was abused, my memory is pretty darn sharp. I would think that's true for most victims of abuse; their recollections of suffering are eidetic and palpable, so much so that sometimes we stand so close to our memories that we can't see past them. I'm not going to pull any punches because you, the reader, need to feel and understand what being bullied is like, and what it does to people, especially children.

All I can do, in the end, is put the story in front of you. After you read this book, if it affects you, I hope you will make a decision to do something. It might mean literally intervening on behalf of a child you suspect is being bullied. It might mean attending a meeting at your child's school on bullying that you weren't planning to attend before you read this book. It might not make a difference, but then again, it might prevent a suicide for a kid who sees his predicament as insolvable. It could be that important. If you read this book and agree with me, I hope you'll do something about it.

1

It was shortly after ten o'clock on a warm Sunday morning, on June 20, 2010. The news on television was mostly bad and depressing, bombs going off in Baghdad and an uncapped British Petroleum oil well belching black clouds of oil into the Gulf of Mexico. It was Father's Day, but I was not a father, nor had I ever had a reason to celebrate Father's Day—or, for that matter, Mother's Day. I'd driven six hours south from my home in Salt Lake City, Utah, because I wanted—because I *needed*—to get away from it all. And by "it all," I meant "people."

In that regard, I was successful. I could hardly have been farther away from people than here, navigating a crack in the earth, an hour from the closest town of Page, Arizona. I'd been moving at a good pace since breakfast, traveling down one of the Colorado Plateau's slot canyons, a unique topography created by hydrological and aeolian forces that over the eons had eroded the red sandstone surrounding me. Slot canyons are like knife slices in the earth, and some can be hundreds of feet deep and only a few feet wide. The canyon I was in (and this was the reason I chose it) was a technical canyon, meaning it could not be traversed without the use of ropes and climbing gear: carabiners, a harness, ascenders, bolts, and anchors. I was traveling down from the head of the canyon, the first mile or so an easy stroll on a sandy path, but then the adventure began. Each time I had to set my ropes and rappel down, a skill I learned in the Marines, I increased the danger, because without my gear, I would not be able to turn around and exit the way I entered, or go forward beyond the next technical traverse, and gear can always fail. Humans are more likely to fail than gear; one bad bolt-set or hastily tied knot, and I could find myself at the bottom of a hole with no way out. I'd applied pre-mission preparation procedures drilled into me in the Marine Corps. I'd built in as many precautions as possible, brought more rope than I expected I'd need, and I'd given my wife, Michelle, my location and a "drop dead" time, meaning that if she didn't hear from me by then, she should call search and rescue. Even that didn't mean I'd be safe.

Michelle worries because I prefer to explore places like this alone. The risk I face, and enjoy, exploring solo has changed little since the days when mountain men and fur trappers blazed trails in this forlorn part of the globe—if you mess up, you're screwed. A broken leg or even a twisted ankle can leave you trapped somewhere no one will think to look for you. Canyoneers must also concern themselves with flash floods, particularly in the secondary and tertiary canyons that feed into the Grand Canyon and the Colorado River. In a wider canyon, if you have enough warning of a flash flood, there are often places you can run to where you may be able to scramble up to higher ground. In a slot canyon like this, there's no way out, no way up without climbing gear, and no way to ride out a flood when constrictions amplify the force of the water. In the summer of 1997, twelve people were trapped in Antelope Canyon, perhaps the best known and easily the most traveled slot canyon in the Four Corners region, by a flood resulting from a storm ten miles upstream where the catchment saw an inch and a half of rain, with three-quarters of an inch falling in only fifteen minutes. Downstream in Antelope Canyon, it barely drizzled, a few drops falling, until, half an hour later, a surge of water ten feet high raced down the canyon, destroying everything and everyone in its path.

I chose to explore alone to get away from people and to test myself. I didn't necessarily think that other people would either slow me down or annoy me; going solo simply meant having a more pleasant journey without any awkward moments with new partners or arguments about which way to go or how to set something up. The challenge is to be self-reliant. Some people find it difficult to be self-reliant. I have never had a choice. I am self-reliant to a fault, and if I could go back in time to reverse the course of events that have made me so, I would, but . . . I can't do that, so I will only play the cards life has dealt me as best I can.

After my second rappel, I stopped to eat a snack and to rest, washing down a Clif Bar with a few gulps of bottled water. After my third rappel, a descent of perhaps twenty feet, I left my ropes in place and paused to examine the gear in my pack to see what I had left. Of the eight twenty-five-foot sections of CMC Static Pro 3/8" diameter climbing rope I brought, I had one section left.

I dropped my pack and headed down-canyon. I had Petzl ascenders and both locking and non-locking carabiners clipped to my Yates harness. My bolts and anchors and my DeWalt cordless drill were in the pack. I could come back if I needed them, but I was of the mind that if the next obstacle I reached presented too much of a challenge, I'd call it a day and turn around. At some point, the lure of what's around the next corner is cancelled out by the trouble it's going to take to get back, but whenever I stop for the day, it's generally not with a sense of disappointment, but more with one of accomplishment. It's that point when you think, "I've come this far alone safely; don't push it."

I walked about fifty yards down to where the canyon narrowed, the walls only a few yards apart, rising perhaps three hundred feet above me, though they curved and leaned and I couldn't see the top. The sun was no longer directly overhead. It was noticeably cooler as I passed through shadows dark enough that I occasionally had to turn on my headlamp to see the smaller details. The streambed underfoot was sandy for the most part but, in the low depressions that held standing water before eventual evaporation, the sand had caked into tiles of mud that curled at the edges and crunched with each step I took. The sound brought me back to winters and springs, growing up in Wisconsin. I found it pleasing, similar to stomping on the ice crusted at the edge of the snow banks lining the streets in my hometown.

Ahead, I saw daylight where the canyon opened up again. I looked up. The walls loomed above me, as if threatening to collapse. I estimated that from where I started my day, I'd come about two miles, horizontal.

I regarded the sweep of the striated sandstone walls, red and brown, tan and yellow. It was beautiful, and I was glad I came. For a moment, I pretended I was the first man who ever set foot here. I chose this canyon from an old out-of-print guidebook because the description made it sound like a place too difficult to visit, meaning it would be untrammeled by day-tourists in flip-flops. I'd read where they've found large amounts of human garbage washed up on the beaches of deserted islands in the middle of the Pacific Ocean. For me, finding a candy wrapper or a soda can in a canyon I'm exploring was always more than disappointing—it felt like falling off the wagon, in a way, a setback in my ongoing struggle to be more optimistic about people.

A brief and admittedly amateur accounting of the geology of Utah can explain how the slot canyons of Southern Utah and Northern Arizona formed. At various times over the eons, the mountains in the northern part of the state, including the Wasatch, Raft River, and Uinta ranges, were the only part above sea level, and the rest was submerged. The warm seas encroached and receded over a relatively flat topography to the west of the Wasatch line and left thick deposits of sediments, including shale, sandstone, and limestone up to three miles thick. Much of that rock contains marine fossils. Eventually, around the time of the dinosaurs, the seas dried up, turning southern Utah into a vast sandy desert, and that sand became the red rock formations found today in the national parks. Land masses compressed and crashed into each other, creating faults and uplifts and folds and eventually the Rocky Mountains, with swamps and large, lazy rivers draining the coastal plains. Uplifts formed basins, which became lakes and lake beds. Then, about forty million years ago, widespread volcanic activity erupted, leaving thick blankets of volcanic rocks and lava and ash. About twenty million years ago, the part of North America west of the Rockies lifted up out of the sea to present-day elevations, land flowing east and west from the Continental Divide, and the water that had before flowed slowly in lazy rivers now flowed rapidly down steeper slopes, carving into the landforms and refilling the basins. In the high mountains, glaciers formed to sculpt the topography, and then the climate warmed up, the ice receded, and most of the lakes evaporated. Great Salt Lake is one of the last to do so.

The slot canyons of southern Utah and Northern Arizona are evidence of erosion as rainwater sought the shortest path to the sea after the final continental uplift. The most dramatic and most developed is, of course, the Grand Canyon, which is hardly a slot anymore, but at some point in time, around twenty million years ago, it started as one. Walking down into a canyon, big or small, feels like walking backward through time, as marked by the striations on the contoured canyon walls distinguishing different periods of sediment deposits.

Biologically, a slot canyon is a niche most plant and animal species find inhospitable. Very little sunlight reaches the bottom of slot canyons, and when it does, it doesn't stay long. In the canyons that are the most popular with tourists, the best time to go if you want to take pictures is an hour either side of noon, when you can capture rays of sunlight striking the canyon floor, but it's also the worst time to go because that's when everybody goes. At that point, you can't take a picture without taking a picture of somebody else taking a picture. Early morning or late afternoon, you can have the place all to yourself.

Without sunlight, little grows in a slot canyon, maybe a bit of moss somewhere below a shelf where it stays damp and shaded. You might see snakes, scorpions, stink beetles, black flies, and you can see quite a number of birds that build homes on the walls where predators cannot reach them, marked by smears of white bird guano striping the walls below their nests. You can estimate the high water mark in a slot canyon by where the birds build their nests. I've hiked in slot canyons where I've passed under logjam thirty and forty feet overhead, left by flash floods.

I walked and scrambled over fallen rocks for a quarter mile along a winding corridor, descending another fifty feet of elevation, until I reached what I knew would be my final rappel, a fifteen-foot drop over a ledge and down a chute leading to what appeared to be a somewhat deep pothole. Beyond the pothole, a rise of about five feet. What was on the other side of that, I couldn't tell. I pulled myself up to the top of the ledge and looked down into the hole.

I saw something, and my heartbeat quickened. The astonishment I felt went beyond mere surprise. There was an immediate surreality, the way you feel when you wake up in the morning and you can't tell where the dream you were having ends and the day begins.

I saw, unless I was hallucinating, a dog.

But that was crazy.

I tried to think of what else it could be. The creature had exaggerated pelvic and shoulder bones protruding from beneath matted black fur. *Maybe a baby calf,* I thought. Maybe it had somehow wandered far from the herd and had gotten trapped. I tried to think of where it might have come from. The closest town of Page, just south of the Utah–Arizona state line and the Glen Canyon Dam, was too far away. The landscape where I entered the canyon was more high desert than cattle or range land, but perhaps there was a ranch nearby, a fence down somewhere.

It felt utterly strange to look at an animal and not know for certain what kind of animal it was. Clearly the thing in the bottom of the hole was suffering from extreme malnutrition and starvation, so emaciated that it didn't look like a dog any more—if that's, in fact, what it was.

"Hey!" I called out softly. I wanted to be gentle to it, and I didn't want to frighten it.

I needn't have worried. It didn't look up or show any sign that it heard me. It only paced back and forth, head down because it didn't have the strength to lift it. It was weakened, desperate, looking for a way out, walking back and forth, as if hoping the rock walls would open up somehow. The pothole was perhaps fifteen feet deep from where I crouched and eight feet across. The rim opposite me was maybe ten feet from the bottom, the hole shaped more like a ladle than a bowl.

The animal's fur was black and caked with mud. I could almost count the vertebrae in his spine. He had only a cavity where the belly should be. I tried to recall the survival training I received as a Marine. I didn't know about dogs, which I finally decided the creature was, but I knew a man can go as long as a month without nutrition and less than a week without water. The mud-caked fur meant there must have been standing water in the hole

7

at some point. My best guess was that the poor creature was in that final stage of starvation. I knew as well that a kind of madness accompanies malnutrition and, in particular, dehydration when it reaches the point that the body can no longer flush itself of toxins, which then affect brain function by causing chemical imbalances. I recalled that my mother used to say she had a "chemical imbalance," though not from dehydration. I had no way of telling how far gone mentally this poor dog was.

The tail hung limp and seemed incapable of wagging. I couldn't tear my eyes away from its shoulder blades and pelvic bones, which were now the most dominant features on its body. As I watched, the animal collapsed, dropping first to its elbows before falling into the dirt, where it lowered its head to the ground and lay motionless. I wondered if it had died, right before my eyes.

I looked up. The canyon walls were too high to see the topmost edge. I was minimally two hundred feet deep—but perhaps twice that. The sky was a broken narrow blue line. I tried but could not for the life of me figure out how this animal arrived here. It surely could not have fallen and survived.

I looked up-canyon to recall how I'd already used seven twenty-five-foot lengths of rope to reach this spot. I'd needed hand lines to navigate several difficult scrambles and had completed two free-hanging rappels—the dog could not have casually ambled away from its owners and made its way here on its own.

I wondered if he'd arrived here by some natural event. Occasionally, exploring places like this, you come across the carcass or skeleton of a dead animal that got washed into the canyon during a flood. I found the body of a coyote once. Slot canyons are generally not full of life, beyond the birds that make their nests on the canyon walls. Slot canyons are typically too dry and bereft of sunlight to support vegetation. Because there is too little to eat, prey species don't come down into slot canyons, which means predators don't frequent them, either. When there is water, it pours through with such force that it would kill any animal—small or large—caught in the current. About a mile up-canyon, I'd passed beneath a large logjam of tree branches wedged between the canyon walls by the force of flood waters. The logjam had been sixty feet above my head.

In other words, the dog could not have tried to ford a shallow wash or arroyo upstream and gotten carried here. It would have been dashed against the walls.

I took a moment to assess the situation. The first task was to identify and evaluate the problem, but I couldn't do that unless I went down into the pothole. I couldn't go down into the pothole without a hand line at the very least, but I couldn't see any way to rig a hand line—nothing to tie off to, no raw materials to arrange as a dead-man's anchor, no logs or rocks. I would need to set a bolt, but my tools to do that were in my backpack, which I'd left behind.

I almost said, "Wait here," though the dog hardly had a choice. It didn't move, but something told me it was still alive. Maybe that was just the hopeful part of me engaging in wishful thinking. If it was still alive, it was alive the way a candle smolders after you blow out the flame, and for a moment, the tip of the wick glows orange.

I set off to retrieve my pack, and as I moved, I arrived at the only conclusion that remained. I recalled the old Sherlock Holmes stories I read as a boy where the great fictional detective says, "When you have eliminated the impossible, whatever remains, however improbable, must be the truth." The conclusion I reached was that the dog did not find his way into the pothole by accident, by wandering, by an act of nature. He was there because someone put him there.

The thought was appalling, and I picked up my pace.

Then I'm running.

I'm running because I'm being chased. I'm thirteen years old, and a kid is following me home from junior high because he wants to hurt me. If I let him, it will be the second time I've been attacked today. I'm not even sure why he's chasing me, because I haven't done anything to him, but I have been identified as an easy target for bullying. It's a label I've worn, and a burden I've carried, since I was five. I'm afraid of everybody, because it's safer than trying to figure out who might be friendly and who might be a bully. Sometimes it feels like I give off some kind of signal that brings out the bully in kids who are never bullies to anybody else, though I can't for the life of me figure out what it is. I'm isolated and alone, because it's not safe for kids who aren't bullies to be seen with me or stick up for me, because then they'd run the risk of getting picked on, too. It is not considered "cool" to stick up for someone who's unpopular. It's like saying you like a band everybody else hates, except, of course, kids who get bullied are not bands.

I can't even remember the first time somebody bullied me. Once, in preschool, somebody called me "stupid head," and everyone else laughed. Was that the first time? Or did I miss the first time? I didn't react, didn't know how to react or realize that I needed to react, and that invited more abuse, because then the goal was to get a reaction from me, the kid who was clueless. Somehow, somewhere, I'd been "chosen" to be the butt of everyone's joke.

I reach the back door of the apartment where I live with my mother, let myself in, and lock the door behind me. I ask myself the same question I've been asking since the bullying first started: "Why is this happening? Why me?" If I knew what the reason was, I could change whatever it is about me that made me so vulnerable to bullying, whatever it is that made me such an inviting target. I'm a normal boy. I'm not weird. I'm not a nerd. I don't smell. I like Star Wars, just like everybody else. I like the same TV shows other kids like. Why have I been singled out? What have I done to deserve it? What did the kids who've escaped bullying do to avoid it—what's the trick?

Somehow, I carry a stigma everywhere I go. When kids choose sides for sports teams at school, I am invariably chosen last, not because I'm a bad athlete, but simply because I'm unpopular. Moving to a different school and starting over is not an option because Cudahy, Wisconsin, does not have school choice, nor could my mother, Sandra, an X-ray technician, make anywhere near enough money to send me to a private school. And even if I went to a new school, I would again be singled out as "the new kid." I understand that some kids are more popular than others, but I am well below merely "unpopular." I am ignored by most people and scorned and abused by others, and I never did anything to hurt anybody.

At home, behind my locked door, I'm safe, but I know I can't go back to school. When my mother gets home from work, I will pretend to be sick, and tomorrow morning, I'll say I have a stomachache. I will not tell her what's happening at school, because I can't talk to her. To be honest, I don't even know if she cares about my troubles. And if I did tell her, she would probably blame me for doing something wrong. I'm safe, temporarily, but I'm still terrified, because I know that the abuse I've been suffering is not going to end. It's not going to get better, and, very likely, it's going to get worse.

I ran for my pack, thinking about a dog that was alone, abandoned, abused, isolated, left for dead by someone. I didn't know who, and I couldn't say why, but I knew, I was certain, what the dog was feeling. Our paths had crossed, and now we were connected, either by destiny or random chance, but from the moment I first saw him, I knew I wanted to prove something to him—that even though some other human had done this to him, this one wasn't like that.

In that moment, I also knew I was not going to leave him where he was, or pretend I hadn't seen what I saw, or that it was not my

Zachary Anderegg

responsibility to save him. That part was almost simple. I didn't need to ask, *Could I live with myself, if I didn't do something to save him? Would I ever be able to get the image out of my head of the poor creature, abandoned at the bottom of a hole?* The easy answer to both questions was no.

I retrieved my pack. For the first time since leaving Salt Lake City, I wished I wasn't alone. I returned to the pothole, took out my cordless drill, notched a drill bit, and tightened the chuck. I picked a spot in the rock at the top of the chute and began to drill, setting my bit at an angle perpendicular to the rock face. After about thirty seconds, my bit was perhaps six inches into the soft sandstone, deep enough to set a bolt and hanger. I took a bolt from my pack, a five-inch-long threaded zinc screw with a sleeve around the threads, pounded it in with my hammer, and tightened it with a wrench, turning it several full rotations clockwise. The hanger attached to the bolt compressed between the sandstone and the nut, locking up tight. I clipped into it and tested it. It seemed secure, but if I was wrong, I could find myself in the same predicament the dog was in: trapped without food or water.

I put on my climbing gloves, leather with padded palms for grip and protection from friction, and backed down the chute hand-over-hand. I felt the air turn damp and several degrees cooler as I descended. The bottom of the pothole sloped down-canyon, and at the lower end, there was a layer of damp mud.

I knelt down next to the dog. His eyes were open, but he didn't look at me. He stared off into nothing, listless and unresponsive. I took off my gloves and laid my hand on his side. I could feel his ribs, hardly any muscle tissue between them, and the ends felt sharp, as if they could perforate his skin. I couldn't feel a heartbeat, but his rib cage expanded, barely, as he breathed. I tried to give him an affectionate touch, a scratch behind the ears, but he was

12

unresponsive and motionless. I wondered how he'd summoned the strength to walk in circles when I first saw him.

Now it was as if he knew I was there, and he was giving himself over to me.

"You're going to be all right," I said softly. "I'm going to get you out of here."

Was I trying to convince myself or the dog?

I found my water bottle and unscrewed the cap. I positioned the mouth of the bottle close to the dog's lips. Suddenly he lifted his head and opened his mouth to display his teeth, one last effort to defend himself, perhaps, but when he tried to growl, I heard only a rasp. His head went down again. It was all he could do.

I poured some water onto the rock in front of his mouth. He didn't notice.

"Come on," I said. "You have to drink something."

I poured more water in front of his mouth, splashing it onto his lips, but again, no response. I considered pouring water directly into his mouth, though I feared he might gag on it or even drown. Then, when I accidentally spilled water onto his paw, directly in front of his face, he seemed to understand what I was offering him for the first time. His eyes moved slowly. His small tongue came out, dry and almost white, and he licked the top of his paw, but in slow motion, his tongue absorbing the water like a sponge before he transferred it to his mouth and throat.

That deep in the canyon, no surface sounds penetrated. The angles of the rock walls formed acoustic baffles to dampen any noise. In the quiet, above the sound of my own breathing and maybe the pounding of my heart, I heard his stomach gurgling. One drip at a time, I put water on his paw and he lapped at it.

I was encouraged, but his extreme weakness and frailty concerned me. I had no medical training, but even so, it seemed clear to me that I couldn't put him in my backpack and take him out the way I came. He would not survive the journey. On the side of the pothole, opposite the mud, I noticed a half dozen pieces of desiccated feces, white and flaky. How long had this poor creature been trapped?

His neck went limp. The simple act of licking his paw drained him. I looked up. The thin strip of sky I saw was cloudless and blue. I had checked the weather report that morning before entering the canyon. No chance of rain, it said. No danger from flooding, or from predators, or cave-ins, or collapses. Time was now the dog's only enemy. He needed water, and he needed food, and for some reason, I chose this day to enter this canyon and find him, so it was up to me.

Once again, long buried memories flooded back.

I am hiding in my bedroom, wishing someone would come find me and ask me what's wrong, but knowing they won't. Part of me doesn't want anyone to find me because I feel profoundly ashamed. I am utterly humiliated, and I know of all people, my mother will not be able to help me if I tell her what's going on. She can't even help herself. And what would I tell her? That I'm obviously screwed up in some way. That there's something about me that everyone simply likes to hate. I have nowhere safe to go. What good would sharing any of that do me? So I just learn to keep it all inside. And I learn how to hide . . . everything.

Kneeling beside the dog, I placed my hand on his head and stroked it, curling my finger against his cheek. His stare was blank, focused on infinity. I couldn't say for certain if he could hear me, and I knew he wouldn't understand my words, but if he could still understand anything, I thought, it would be touch. I leaned in close, stroked his head and said, "You're not alone anymore." I think what I really meant was *we're* not alone anymore.

2

The trip back to my campsite at the head of the canyon took a little more than an hour, less than the time I logged getting in because I'd left my lines in place for the return trip, and because now I was racing against the clock. Near the pothole, I set a coil of rope on a ledge where I hoped I'd be able to see it from the top of the canyon; it was the only way I could think of to mark the spot. It was clear to me that the fastest and safest way to get the dog out of the hole (though it would be the most difficult approach for me) would be a vertical drop from as close to the pothole as I could get. The horizontal distance from the pothole to the head of the canyon was maybe two miles, but the technical sections, the drops I had to rappel and the obstacles I had to scramble over to get here, would be too dangerous for the dog, even in a protective crate or sling.

Back at my truck, I left everything in place and five minutes later was headed off in my ATV for a nearby village, bouncing along the washboard gravel road with only my wallet and my cell phone in my pockets. I wanted to call Michelle to fill her in, but coverage near the canyon was spotty at best and time was of the essence. I knew she'd understand when I finally did get hold of her.

I pulled into the parking lot of a convenience store, wondering who could help me. Perhaps there was some sort of volunteer search-and-rescue organization in the area, I thought, though it seemed unlikely that they'd bother saving a small dog trapped in a deep canyon. I knew that, in the recent past, National Park Service policy had begun to rescue stranded hikers or mountain climbers—but then they'd send them the bill for the rescue operation, generally a number in four figures, partly to deter ill-prepared campers and climbers from taking undue risks and partly to recoup costs. Given the recent struggle my business in Salt Lake City had been having making ends meet, I wasn't prepared to bear the burden. I wasn't even sure if fire departments still rescued cats from trees. I doubted anybody was going to send a helicopter or a National Guard unit to save a puppy.

In the grocery store, I bought four cans of wet dog food with pop-top lids, a small bag of dry food, and a package of small Styrofoam bowls from the picnic supply section. I purchased bottled spring water to refill my canteens and then paused at a bulletin board by the front door. Among the notices for tag sales, landscapers, and home repair services, I could find nothing about a lost dog. I asked a few locals in the parking lot if they knew of anyone who lost a dog, but no one seemed to know anything—or care. I knew it then: No one was going to help me—I had to do this by myself.

This is what I meant when I said I'm self-reliant to a fault. It's a habit of mine, but it's also a coping mechanism. As a Marine, I learned to take care of my team members, but I also learned to take care of myself as much as possible, so that my fellow Marines didn't have to take care of me.

I decided before heading back to the canyon I would check in with Michelle, given that I now had signal. She answered in a tone she always uses when I call from out in the desert; real upbeat, like she hasn't spoke to me in a month. I always give her a hard time about it.

"You won't believe what I found out here."

"What?" she asked.

"I found a little black puppy stuck in a pothole. I've never seen an animal in such bad shape. It's just awful."

"Oh my God, what are you going to do?" The words came out of her mouth but she already knew I was going to try to get him out.

"I just picked up some things at the store and I'm going to go leave some food for him. I'll go into Page this afternoon and try to find a carrier or something to get him out of there."

My voice was a bit sharp, filled with disgust for the situation. Michelle knows me well and understood my mood. We both have a love for animals, but when a situation involves some type of cruelty or abuse, I definitely go to a darker place, a place filled with hatred and resentment for those who exercise their power in ways that hurt, even kill.

I told her if she didn't hear from me by sundown then something went wrong. She told me to be safe and we said our goodbyes.

I remounted my ATV, supplies in hand, and headed back to the canyon.

As the landscape flies past me, I'm standing on a corner, waiting for a bus in Cudahy, Wisconsin, a suburb of Milwaukee. Every morning, I stand on the curb and stare down the street in the direction the bus will come, and as I wait for the bus, I fill with dread, an ever-tightening knot in my stomach that makes me feel like I'm going to throw up. Every morning, I rehearse what I'll do, depending on what seats are available, though the bus picks up the same kids in the same order each day, presenting the same set of problems. The best seat, the safest place to sit, is the front row just behind the driver, with some harmless kids directly behind me as a buffer. The real threat is in the back of the bus, where the mean kids sit to be the farthest from the driver. In the worst case scenario, I get on the bus and walk down the aisle, and I see open places, but kids usually have their bags there, and they don't move them for me. Their actions say, loud and clear, "Not here—I don't want a loser like you sitting next to me." But I have to sit down or the bus won't move. On those occasions, I'm forced to sit near the back, amid the boys who might slap me, or thwack the back of my head with a finger, or pop their hands over my ears, or call me names.

Friday nights and Saturdays offer relief, but Sundays, the knot in my gut tightens, because I'm worried about Monday, when it starts all over again. The bus driver is essentially powerless, occasionally glancing in his rear-view mirror and calling out, "Simmer down in the back," but unless backpacks actually fly through the air, he is oblivious to what goes on, his eyes on the road. This is how I start my day. I can't fight back, and I can't flee, so I brace myself, pick a point a few feet in front of me, and stare at it, trying to make myself invisible, and pretending I don't hear them when they call me a queer, or loser, or threaten to kick my ass.

The leaders of the conspiracy are two boys named Wade and Kevin. Kevin clearly doesn't like me. Wade's attitude is more confusing because he will talk to me and be almost friendly, but only if we're alone and somewhere no one else can see us. In public, he gets laughs by making fun of me. The bus ride is a free-for-all, where abuse can come from almost anybody. It feels like it's organized somehow, like they have regularly scheduled "Let's pick on Zak Anderegg" meetings where they decide who's going to take which shift.

I see bullied kids on television, on the sitcom reruns I sometimes watch after school. On television, bullying is generally depicted as comical, the wimpy boy who gets turned upside down and deposited *in a trash can, and maybe he gets an "atomic wedgie" to the delight of his friends and peers, while the laugh track howls with glee and mirth. It's not like that in real life, not even close. It's never funny to the person being picked on. It always hurts, even when you pretend it doesn't or laugh at yourself or put yourself down first to preempt further put-downs. The first instance scars you. Subsequent events deform and cripple you. Every time you're picked last for a team, you feel your ears burning with embarrassment, and when the coach or gym teacher instructs the class to choose up sides, you try to hide behind somebody else as a way to save face, or prepare an excuse, telling yourself, "The reason I was picked last was because the captains couldn't see me." Every time you hear kids talking about an after-school event they're attending, you know you won't be invited so you walk away quickly to pretend you couldn't hear, or you make up a story and say you have to go straight home after school, but even so, when you're not invited, you want to cry. You don't pull yourself out of the garbage can, dust yourself off, and laugh about what just happened to you, hardy har har. You develop a hyper-vigilant mindset, because you're on display all the time, conspicuous and singled out as you try to ward off an insidious sense of constant betrayal, where you don't know who your real friends are or where or when your enemies are going to pull something.*

Even on the bus, on my way to school, there are, in fact, a few kids who'll talk to me or hang out with me or even have me over to their house, but in public, they avoid my company because they want to stay out of the line of fire. They might feel sorry for me, but it's safer for them to not speak up or defend me. I'm a target. Getting too close to me would make them targets, and no one wants to be in my position. I am effectively emotionally quarantined externally by the people who hurt me or exclude me while internally I quarantine myself when I avoid eye contact, speak to no one, pretend to read a book—pretend I like it this way. Pretend I don't need friends . . .

Driving back to the canyon, I knew that, to an extent, I am still this way. At thirty-three—almost thirty-four—years old, I am still that scared little boy. A study in the March 2013 issue of *JAMA Psychiatry* by a scientist at Johns Hopkins said, "The experience of bullying in childhood can have profound effects on mental health in adults," and that adults who were bullied as children are more likely to have anxiety or panic disorders and are almost five times as likely to experience depression. Upon reading this, I wasn't surprised—I grew up not trusting anybody, and certainly not relying on anybody. Today, I am initially distrustful of people, and I often expect the worst from them,

Or maybe I'm just surprised when something short of "the worst" happens. When I become someone's friend, they could not wish for a friend more loyal or committed, but I am slow to commit, wary and skeptical. It explains in part why I so quickly committed to helping the dog—it was not a commitment that required questioning, so I could make it without hesitation.

Back at my truck, I parked the ATV, a 4WD Yamaha Grizzly. I realized I was going to have to make an exception to my rule to ride only on designated dirt roads and ATV trails. I transferred the supplies I'd bought to my backpack, then fastened it to the cargo rack on the ATV and headed toward the canyon rim, bouncing over the depressions and steering to avoid the larger rocks and clumps of sagebrush and mesquite. I had to guess where the pothole would be, and I knew I could be off by a half mile in either direction.

Finally I stopped the ATV and walked to the edge of the canyon, stepping down the decline as far as I dared, looking for the coiled rope I'd left as a marker. I didn't see it. I walked twenty yards toward the head of the canyon and looked again.

There it was.

This was dumb luck, but, I thought, *I'll take it.*

I scouted around for something to anchor to, but the ground was too loose and sandy to set a bolt. I made a decision I hoped I wouldn't regret and decided to use my ATV as an anchor. A Yamaha Grizzly weighs more than six hundred pounds and would be nearly impossible to drag while in park, but to be safe, I tied both hand brakes in the engaged position and chocked all four wheels with large stones to avoid some sort of accidental Wile E. Coyote scenario where I plunged to the bottom of the canyon and pulled my ATV down on top of me.

I tied a 200-foot length of rope to a 265-foot length with a figure-eight joining knot, calculating that had to be more than enough length. I fastened one end to the ATV, backed my anchor up in two places with redundant knots (in case the first one failed), and then tossed the coil over the edge and watched my line fall clear. I clipped on to begin my descent, giving the rope as firm a tug as I could to test it before loading it. If I looked calm and collected from the outside, inside I was terrified, making what was probably going to be the longest rappel of my life, knowing that a fall meant certain (and sudden) death, and that if I hurt myself or miscalculated and for some reason couldn't get out the way I got in, I could face a death less sudden but no less final.

Fifty feet down, the rope brought me over a ridge to a hundred-foot free drop and then a ledge where I could rest a minute, dividing my descent into two stages. I leaned out, but I still couldn't see the bottom. I passed the figure-eight knot through my descender and kept going, careful to avoid kicking any loose rocks that could fall on the dog below. Another hundred feet and I was down, hitting the canyon floor about twenty feet upstream from the pothole.

When I reached the dog, he didn't turn his head or look up or wag his tail, but he was still breathing. I realized I'd been bracing myself for the possibility that I'd get back and find him dead, in which case I would have pulled him out and given him a proper burial, but he was hanging on to life with whatever strength he had left. My goal and hope, bringing him food and water, was to make him stronger, even if only by the smallest degree. I wondered if, at this stage in the pathology of starvation, he was drifting in and out of consciousness or incompletely aware of what was going on around him. He didn't seem to know I was there.

I crouched next to him, cracked the pull tab, and popped open a can of dog food. The smell rising from the contents of the can, strong and putrid, made me gag, but when I held the can under the dog's nose, it acted like smelling salts and revived him. The dog lifted his head, eyes barely open, and extended his tongue to lick the lid. I knew that humans who go on extended fasts feel hungry for the first few days, but then the hunger feeling goes away and sometimes they have to be force-fed to start eating again. How I would manage that with the dog was beyond me. I emptied the dog food into a Styrofoam bowl, set it in front of him, and was gladdened to see I wouldn't have to force him to eat. He took a big bite and swallowed.

Almost immediately, his body began to convulse; he hunched forward as he retched involuntarily. After a half dozen convulsions, he stopped, and thankfully the food stayed down. I pulled the dish away to give him a moment to recover, and then I sat with him and fed him slowly.

I'm fourteen and in my high school cafeteria at a table by the door. I am sitting alone. Everyone who comes in or out of the lunchroom sees me sitting by myself. They see me, but they don't know what I'm thinking. What I'm thinking is this: Who am I? Why am I so worthless?

Every day, I bring a bag lunch and take my sandwich out and look at it and keep my head down, perfecting my thirty-inch stare, while all around me people are laughing and socializing and yelling, the usual chaos of a high school cafeteria. I'm not a stranger or a new kid. Cudahy, Wisconsin, is a suburb of Milwaukee but it feels like a small town where everybody knows everybody. It's a small school, only about seven hundred students. Everybody knows me, but everybody also knows my label. Sitting by myself every day is in-my-face proof that I'm worthless. I am unwanted. I do not dare ask to sit with anybody because if they say no, that would be even more humiliating. And no one wants to sit with me because it's just easier not to. And safer. Anyone sitting with me risks being labeled a loser, too.

I look around the cafeteria and wonder why everybody else is smart enough to figure out how to be in a group. The jocks have groups. The really pretty girls have groups and sub-groups of not-as-pretty girls who act as entourages to the really pretty girls. Every ethnic minority has its own minority group. There's even a group of unpopular kids—a group for kids who don't have a group—but they don't seem to want me either. If I gathered the courage to ask, I wonder if they'd let me join them, but I don't try, because it would be too embarrassing if they rejected me, too. The loneliness I feel is merciless, and the message comes across clear as a bell: "You're on your own."

I let the dog eat and didn't try to pet him, but I sat with him to let him know someone was there. Buck Brannaman, the horse trainer on whom both the book and the movie *Horse Whisperer* were based, never had to use physical pain to discipline his horses because he understood that the pain of isolation was worse and that depriving an animal of the safety and security of its social community was a more powerful negative reinforcement than any spur or whip. I sat with the dog, thinking that dogs are social animals, just like horses, and that unless he'd learned to mistrust humans entirely, my presence might comfort him. When he stopped eating, not because he'd had enough but because, I assumed, what was left of his atrophied stomach couldn't hold any more, he moved to the drinking water I'd poured in a bowl for him. He took slow, deliberate laps of water. I wasn't exactly sure why I felt the need, but I decided to shoot some video footage of him to document his condition and perhaps to help me process, later, what I was experiencing. It wasn't making sense now, but maybe it would upon further contemplation.

Shortly after partaking of food and water, the dog collapsed. It reaffirmed what I'd surmised earlier: he was too frail to carry out of the canyon the easy way. He was small, so his weight wasn't the issue—I guessed he was maybe five months old and weighed about seventeen pounds, soaking wet. What I feared was the act of simply placing him in my backpack and climbing back out. His positioning inside (scrunched up and folded over himself), paired with possible jostling as I worked quickly to get him out of there, could have resulted in broken bones and other probable traumas. I was going to have to lift him in some kind of crate, straight up and out of the canyon.

I hollowed out five depressions in the soft caked mud at the bottom of the pothole and then set a Styrofoam bowl in each, testing to make sure the dog wouldn't be able to tip the bowls over and spill the contents. When I was satisfied, I filled three bowls with water and two with dog food. I briefly worried that the strong aroma of the dog food would attract predators, or perhaps vultures from high above who might see the dog and think they wouldn't have to wait very long for a meal, but it was a risk I couldn't avoid. I had to trust that the bottom of a slot canyon was the last place any creature in the food chain was going to look for sustenance.

I looked up, out of instinct, to gauge how much daylight I had left, even though from the bottom of a slot canyon, it's impossible to tell time that way. I looked at my watch. It was a little after 4:30 p.m. I took a blue towel from my pack, one I carry for those occasions when a lake or stream presents me with the opportunity to bathe, set it on the canyon floor folded in half, then moved to where the dog was lying. I slid my hands under him and gently lifted. He was almost literally a bag of bones. If he were healthy, I thought, he ought to weight thirty or more pounds, but he was light as a kitten and limp in my hands. I set him down carefully on the center of the towel, which would insulate him from the cold mud that would otherwise conduct heat away from his body. It was hard to understand how he hadn't already succumbed to hypothermia, sleeping for however many days down here. If he had the strength, the food and water were there for him.

"I'll be back tomorrow morning," I told him. "I promise."

I wondered what the sound of my voice did for him. I wondered if he could tell that today had been better than yesterday, and tomorrow would be better than today. I could clearly recall days when nobody could have convinced me of that, but perhaps this was where my human intelligence and the dog's diverged. Humans who experience trauma learn from it, over and over again, reviewing the traumatic experience and reliving it as a memory, carrying the pain and the hurt over from one day to the next. I wondered how the canine intelligence handles something like this—how traumatized would the dog be? Would he be mentally and emotionally damaged, even if he recovered his physical health, or would he find a way to forget?

On my way back up the rope, I negotiated the free-hangs and the ledges and, in perhaps fifteen minutes, maybe less, I was back at the top. My arms were weary. How was I going to do the same climb tomorrow with the dog in tow? I would have to find a way.

On the hour-long drive back to Page, I thought of how the dog's life was now in my hands. I had a responsibility to him. I didn't choose it, but I couldn't turn away from it, either. As I drove, an ember of anger burned inside me. The more I thought about it, the more certain I was that the dog at the bottom of the canyon did not arrive there by accident. Someone put him there quite intentionally.

I considered, again, the obstacles I had to overcome to find him in the first place, a twenty-foot free-hanging rappel and a ten-foot sheer wall at an eighty-degree incline in pitch blackness. No. The dog did not wander down the canyon on his own—he would have broken a leg at the very least. He did not get washed to where I found him in a flood—he would have been dashed against the rocks or, surviving that, he would have drowned while treading water in the pothole.

Someone put him there.

I couldn't stop thinking about who would do such a thing. Why would they do it?

It made no sense. I could imagine—not that this made *sense* exactly—how someone, for whatever twisted reason, might be cruel to an animal as a kind of hands-on experience, where there's some kind of pleasure derived from the animal's tortured reaction. In Elizabethan England, they used to bait bears by chaining a bear to a stake and then worrying it with dogs as a kind of public spectacle, and people would cheer, the way (I assume) they cheer today at dog fights or cock fights. In the Roman Colosseum, thousands of years ago, spectacles of pure cruelty were near-daily invents.

But there was no element of spectacle to the dog in the canyon, nobody there to savor the animal's suffering. There were no witnesses. In fact, you could hardly find a place less likely to ever have witnesses. Whoever had done it did so hoping not to be caught. No one could derive pleasure from the dog's reaction, except conceptually. How long would it take to kill a dog by starving it? However long it was, there was no immediate return, no instant gratification.

I could even explain finding a dog in that condition as a result of neglect, somebody who, for example, leaves a dog in a house and never goes back and somehow manages to banish from his or her thoughts any recollection of leaving behind a pet without food—but neglect is a passive kind of cruelty. It's a crime of omission, a lack of action. The dog in the canyon had not been passively neglected.

Someone had gone to a great deal of trouble to put it there. Someone used ropes and climbing gear, as I had, to reach the pothole where I found the dog. The dog was probably lowered by rope over the difficult sections, all an enormous effort to get a dog down there. Someone had quite intentionally, with planning and malice aforethought and with considerable exertion, brought the dog deep into the canyon and left it there to die.

I am fourteen. I am in my room, sitting on my mattress on the floor. My mother is in the living room, but she is beyond reach, inaccessible, the last person I could possibly turn to. I am absolutely alone, and nothing is going to change, and I think that all I really want is for the pain I feel to stop, and the only way I can imagine it stopping is if I was dead. I, too, have been left to die. At the age of fourteen, the idea of being dead has considerable appeal. I would not do it to spite anyone or hurt anyone, only to end the misery. Sometimes it feels as if I have no other way out.

3

Back in Page, teenagers on bicycles loitered in front of the convenience stores, their curfews approaching, probably talking about how boring their lives were, because that's what teenagers everywhere think—especially on a Sunday when nothing is open, and even more so when it's summer, which seems to last forever when you're a teenager. Old people at the other end of their lives clogged the streets with their lumbering RVs, which I found frustrating because I needed to reach the fire station as soon as possible. I didn't know where else to ask for help—going to the police station seemed too extreme. It seemed reasonable to expect that in an area with so much surrounding wilderness, there could have been some kind of volunteer search-and-rescue organization or unit to get advice from, if not actual assistance. I wasn't sure how much assistance I could expect from the fire department, given that I was only rescuing a dog, but you see stories all the time about heroic firemen rescuing cats from trees. I hoped I'd be able to persuade them, though it seemed unlikely they'd care as much as I did.

The fire station, a nondescript brick and glass building with three large bays in the front for fire engines, was next to the police station on Coppermine Road, just down from the Motel 6, where a sign said there was a vacancy. Ordinarily, I prefer to camp in the truck, but tonight I decided to get a room, to prepare. I parked in a nearly empty parking lot, hoping that someone would be inside to offer assistance. As I walked into the fire station, I considered how I would plead my case and thought I might spin it a bit and mention what great publicity it would be for whoever helped me.

The lobby was empty, but there was a red telephone on a desk next to a sign that said "Please Call for Assistance." A woman answered, and when I told her the reason for my visit, she told me to hang on and someone would be out shortly.

A minute later, a kid who looked like he was in his mid-twenties, with a buzz cut that reminded me of my time in the Marines, came out and asked me nonchalantly what was up. He was wearing a navy blue T-shirt and baggy firefighting pants held up by yellow and silver reflective suspenders.

"I was in a canyon today, about an hour from here," I said, telling him where it was, "and I found a dog in a pothole, and I think he's going to die if we can't get him out."

"Okay," he said.

"I was wondering if you had any thoughts."

"If I have any thoughts?"

"Yeah."

"Well," he said, "we can't really send out the manpower and the equipment you'd need to do that. We have to be on standby if we get a call to a fire."

"That makes sense," I told him, and it did, but it was disappointing. "Is there any sort of volunteer search-and-rescue group I could contact?"

"In Page?"

"Yeah."

"Not in Page. That I know of."

"What do you do if someone gets lost in the Grand Canyon?"

"That's the Park Service. You find the dog in a National Park?"

"No."

"Sorry."

I could tell that he really was. He was still trying to think of a way to help me, but he was coming up empty. I thanked him anyway.

"You going in yourself?"

"I guess," I said.

"You know what you're doing?"

"I think so," I said. "If I screw it up and get stuck myself, then will you come get us both?"

"Sure," he said.

"Don't worry—that's not part of the plan," I said, though it occurred to me that if all else failed, it could be. "Is there an animal hospital in town?"

He wrote down the name and the address, gave me directions, and wished me luck. I told him I'd need it.

Page Animal Hospital was a small, single-story white cottage with an addition for offices on the side, on the corner of Eighth and Elm in the center of town. As I parked the truck, I felt relieved, thinking I would at least be getting some kind of good professional advice. The sun was getting lower in the sky, intensifying the light. The front door was open, but the lobby was empty, and the front desk was unoccupied. On a Sunday night, I was happy the door was open. The place was dead quiet. The floor was gray linoleum. Charts on the walls displayed the anatomies of cats and dogs.

When I heard a noise, I called out, "Hello?"

I heard someone shout back, "Just a minute."

A few seconds later, a weathered looking woman in her early fifties came out, a rag in one hand and a spray bottle of Windex in the other. The only help I could get was from the cleaning lady. She told me the doctor would be back in the morning. I briefly described the situation and asked if she knew where I could get some kind of cat or dog carrier to transport the puppy in. She said they had a few I could choose from and led me to a back room, where I selected one of an appropriate size, red plastic with mesh windows and doors and a handle on the top. I asked her if she thought the doctor would be able to treat a sick animal. I knew it was a stupid question—that's what they did.

"Oh sure," she said. "Dr. Roundtree takes all kinds of strays." A diploma on the wall indicated the head veterinarian was a Dr. Jerry Roundtree, DVM.

I thanked her. As she walked me back to the front door, she shared something with me.

"My husband was at the landfill last week. He heard some noises coming from a sofa somebody left. He looked at it. There were eight kittens that got stuffed inside the sofa. They just threw 'em away. A lot of times we get strays that have highway injuries. People around here don't spay. Especially not on the Navajo reservation. So we get a lot of unwanted animals."

I realized my jaw was clenched, and that my disdain for people was surfacing again. Of course, this was in reaction to her news, not to her.

"Thanks for your help," I said. "I'll be in tomorrow."

I went to look for a place to eat, though Page, Arizona, is not exactly the restaurant capital of the Colorado Plateau. If you Google "Page + Arizona + restaurants," you find a single listing for a place called Wahweap's Rainbow Room on Lake Powell. Most of the people who live in Page either work for the Glen Canyon Dam hydroelectric plant, the Navajo power plant, which is coal-fired—you can see the smokestacks for miles—or they work in the tourism industry. There are a lot of great scenic views in Page, but only if you're in town, looking away from town at the distant mesas and buttes burnt red by the sun. Anything you see that's green is the result of irrigation, and everywhere else, it's high desert.

I settled for dinner at McDonald's. I didn't realize how famished I was, and I wanted to ingest the greatest number of calories in the shortest amount of time. It seemed almost obscene that it only took me ten minutes to take in more nourishment than the dog had had in weeks.

Another thing I hadn't realized was how thinking about the dog was evoking memories I thought were buried, resurrecting ancient hurts and sending me on trips into the past I didn't necessarily want to take. For example, while at McDonald's, I saw a kid with red hair and I reflexively recoiled from him—a sign of how I'm scarred. I knew my bias was irrational and unjustified, but Wade, the kid who bullied me when I was in grade school, had red hair. Wade was athletic and had a reputation for being tough, so a lot of people followed him, sensing it was probably smarter to be his friend than his enemy. It's irrational to distrust people with red hair, just because you had a problem with one person who had red hair, but I recognized it as a propensity I had.

Then a girl at McDonald's reminded me of a girl I knew in fifth grade who'd sent me a "love letter." *"Dear Zak, I think you're really cute..."* etcetera. It was a joke, a prank, but I fell for it. I'd known this girl since preschool, and I thought she was particularly smart and confident, and not someone who moved with the popular kids, necessarily, but high enough in the social hierarchy of elementary school to do as she pleased without fear of making herself unpopular. It didn't seem so far-fetched, that she might like me, though in fifth grade, I wasn't sure exactly what that meant. Girls mature more quickly than boys do in this regard. The letter was, apparently, a random joke she decided to play for her own amusement, and then she saw it as an opportunity to humiliate me in front of the class. I wrote her a letter back, a sincere response, and she mocked me for it, read it aloud to her friends, who squealed with delight, and passed my letter around for everyone else to read. I was mortified. She played it out for days.

If I had a good year, it would have been sixth grade, when I became one of the oldest kids in my elementary school, and some of the kids who'd bullied me the previous five years had all moved up to junior high school. For nine months during the school year, I was no longer afraid of leaving the house or getting on the bus. I made a few friends, was able to concentrate in class, and I enjoyed learning about the physical sciences. I even enjoyed the more challenging math that we were being taught. Yet I could not forget, entirely, the way things had been before, and I worried that the relief I felt was only temporary, a kind of false hope, because I knew the older kids who'd bullied me were going to be there when I got to junior high. The closer it got, the more I worried, making my first day of junior high school one of the most dreaded days of my life. Were things going to be different, now that my tormentors had all had a year to mature, or would they simply pick up where they'd left off? Would I be just another student, or would I find myself back at the bottom of the pecking order?

It's the first day of seventh grade. My knees are weak and my legs are rubbery as I walk onto the school block. I've been dreading this moment for weeks, unable to think of anything else, and I am nearly shaking from fear. Some kids from my grade recognize me and laugh at my obvious discomfort. The bell hasn't even rung, and it has begun. My anxiety is supplemented by the usual culture shock kids experience going from an old school to a new one, with lockers that have locks and combinations to learn and memorize (a lot of kids have anxiety about learning to open their lockers, but mine was particularly acute because I felt like if I failed, and the bell rang before I could get my locker open, everyone would notice and laugh at me), and seven different classes in seven different classrooms, and new alliances to form, or in my case, to fear. I'd held out a very small amount of hope that maybe things would be different, and that I'd make new friends who would take me in and protect me, and that I would find my way forward. . . . Instead, I am immediately identified as a loser. For all I know, word has spread about me before school even starts. Nobody volunteers to be my friend, and I'm hesitant to initiate friendships for fear of making a mistake and being rejected, or worse, tricked, like the girl who wrote me the fake love letter. Kids I don't even know avoid me. I feel alone, and that's terrible, but it's still better than being belittled and humiliated. I try, at first, to keep to myself, keep my head down, hoping I'm invisible.

But of course, I'm not invisible, and in a way I can see now but couldn't see then, keeping my head down and trying not to look anybody in the eye signals weakness and serves as an open invitation. My new seventh grade tormentor is a boy named Ben. Ben is the sort of kid who, if you lined up a dozen kids from that school and said, "Pick the biggest loser," would get chosen every time, just from how he looks. He has long greasy hair; is at least twenty pounds overweight; favors black T-shirt, jeans, a black leather jacket; always has heavy-metal blasting in his headphones so loud you can hear it from ten feet away; and all he does, as far as I can tell, is hang out on a street corner, smoking cigarettes. He gets terrible grades and has no interesting personality quirks or characteristics that might redeem him, no sense of humor or way with words that makes him popular, and yet all I can think is that he has a group (The Burnouts, they are called) and I don't, and he bullies me, so if he's a complete loser, but he's still above me, where do I rank? His strength is in numbers. I think I could probably kick his ass, one-on-one, but I know that if I ever take a swing at him, five other Burnouts would jump me and beat the hell out of me.

One day, though I've done nothing to provoke him, he comes after me after school with some of his friends, and I'm certain that everything I've been fearing could happen is about to happen. They see me and call my name and start running toward me, but fortunately I have a good lead on them. I don't look back. For all I know, they took a few steps towards me and stopped, but I run all the way home in fear, and I cut classes for the next two days, and then it's the weekend. I'm hoping that over the weekend, he'll have forgotten about it, but the instant Ben sees me on Monday, he picks up right where he left off.

I realize—you can't make yourself invisible. You can't even make yourself small.

Across the room from me at McDonald's, I saw a father and a son, eating hamburgers and sharing a large order of french fries. They didn't say much, but perhaps that's normal, even in a healthy father-son relationship. I couldn't help wondering what would happen if the kid was getting bullied at school, and he came home and told his father about it.

"What's the name of the boy who's picking on you?" the father would say.

"Ben."

"Why don't I have a little talk with this Ben?" the father would suggest, and then the next day, he'd either corner Ben in the parking lot and threaten him with bodily harm or else just beat the crap out of him. That would be wrong, of course, but it was a satisfying fantasy. It was even more fantastical for me than for most people, because I never had a father I could talk to about my situation in school.

My contact with my father, Mark, was minimal. He was the second oldest of four boys. He and his older brother, Terry, were adopted. His younger brothers, Greg and Rex, were not. His father, Dwaine, was an accountant for the Racine school system if memory serves me correctly, and his mother, Virginia, or Ginny, stayed home and raised the boys while being very active in communal activities. My uncles had fathered two kids each, and held down white-collar jobs, while my father remained blue-collar. The family would all get together for Christmas, and they still do. It struck me as odd that as dysfunctional as my mother's childhood was, my father's was the opposite, and yet he did not come out of it any more prepared to be a parent than my mother had from her family.

Mark was an X-ray technician, like my mother. They met in X-ray technician school. He was twenty-six years old when I was born, younger than my mom was. I have been told they divorced sixteen weeks after I was born. The obvious question then is, was my birth an intentional event, and if it was, was it ever welcomed?

He remarried soon after getting divorced to the woman he'd been having an affair with, according to my mom. Between the ages of four and five, I'd spend Wednesdays and Thursdays at his house with him and his second wife, Robin. She worked at the same hospital as my dad. Robin hated and resented me because I was the living representation of my father's past connection to my mother. Either that or she was just a mean person. She was a cruel, overweight Wisconsin farm girl who was emotionally immature for her age and had a short temper—over two hundred pounds of pure intimidation to a small boy.

All I understood, those first few years that I went there after school, was that she terrified me. When I knew she was coming to pick me up, I'd be so afraid, I'd get physically sick to my stomach. In the car, I'd try not to make eye contact with her and stare out my window.

"There are things to see out my window, too, you know," she'd say, as if she had the right to demand I look in her direction. So I'd time myself, looking out my window for three seconds, then hers for three seconds.

She served cottage cheese all the time, even though she knew I hated it, and she'd make me sit at the table until I finished it. It's not uncommon, I realize, for kids to wrinkle their noses at certain foods, but she'd get up from the table and say, "That better be gone before I get back," and I had good reason to fear her. One time, I saw her go to the door to call the dog in, a husky named Reagan, and when she wouldn't come, I saw Robin grab a section of pipe my father had left by the door and was prepared to throw it at Reagan if she didn't come as called. When Reagan finally came in, she told the dog, "You're lucky you came back," and put the pipe down, but I knew she was prepared to use it.

I spent the afternoons with her, between the time I got home from preschool or kindergarten and when my dad got home, and I'd be on pins and needles. Once I was lying on the floor, pretending I was in a spaceship, and she watched me for a few seconds and then said, "We have toys we bought you in the other room—get them out and play with them right now or I'm going to give them to some kid who wants them."

I couldn't tell my dad about how she treated me because I knew he'd take her side and not mine. He'd tell me I was making things up, or exaggerating, or that I'd misunderstood, or that what I was saying wasn't true, because Robin knew how to hide her behaviors when he was home. The behaviors he did see didn't seem to concern him. I felt, again, that I was alone, and that no one would believe me. How is it possible, I thought, that I could be so scared and miserable, and not one adult could see it?

And suppose I was exaggerating—even if I was over-stating the case—wouldn't a normal parent want to know the reason why I was exaggerating? Even a little kid who thinks there's a monster under his bed and is terrified doesn't want to be scolded and told there's no such thing as monsters under the bed. He's a little kid. He wants to be comforted and sympathized with, and he wants his dad, or his mom, to do something about it.

The kid across the room with his father at McDonald's in Page, Arizona, looked to be about eight, which was about the age I'd reached when the living arrangement changed and I only saw Mark and Robin at Christmas or during holidays. I couldn't say if it was because my mother finally listened to me when I complained and told my father, or if it was because Robin finally convinced him she didn't want me there. Probably some combination of the two.

Then the kid at McDonald's says something, and the father laughs.

I'm fifteen, and my father is driving me back to my mother's house, shortly before Christmas. Things have gotten better between us. As I've gotten older, he has taken more and more of an interest in me. Despite having next to nothing to do with each other, it feels like we've discovered we actually have something in common. He has an ordered curious mind, and his interests are, like mine, more scientific or mechanical than aesthetic or cultural. We talk about how a nuclear cloud would work if the Russians ever attacked America with their missiles. He explains to me how deep sea divers get the bends and why they have to breathe helium under pressure. It's not exactly a heart-to-heart, but I'm impressed by how much he knows. It makes for some novel conversation as we sit in his car for over two hours.

When it's time for me to go inside, he says, "Gimme a hug." I'm shocked to hear this, but I give him a hug, and afterward, it's almost like he's going to cry. He says, "I've been waiting fifteen years for that."

Then I'm twenty-one, and a Marine. My becoming a Marine has clearly impressed him. On our way back from six months of deployment overseas, we're told the ship is going to offer a "Tiger Cruise," from Hawaii to San Diego, where Marines are allowed to invite family members to join them. I invite my father. When we reach Hawaii, he says, "I'm glad you invited me on this trip. This is one of the highlights of my life so far." Being on a large troop ship appeals to his mechanical way of thinking, and he is constantly asking questions about how the ship works. Our relationship seems stronger, sturdier.

But then I'm twenty-nine, about the same age he was when he walked out on my mother and me. I try to put myself in his shoes and understand how someone could abandon a kid, but I can't do it. I ask myself, what would I do if I had a kid? I can't imagine walking away from my own child. The hurt is too deep to let go of, and when I think of what I went through without a father to step in and protect me, or at least advise me while I struggled with all the fear and insecurity and low self-worth, I get angry. There is a great imbalance, and a great injustice, when I feel him expecting loyalty or love from me, as if he'd earned it, or deserves it, after giving me neither for so long. On a subconscious level, I find the idea of a relationship with him less and less acceptable, because he's not saying, "I'm truly sorry for not being there all those years. What can I do to make it up to you?" Rather, he's saying, "Don't ask me to try to make up for the past because I can't. Let's just move forward like things are all rosy." It's about what he can get from me, for free, and it has nothing to do with accepting responsibility for his past actions or for the way he treated me, and it has nothing to do with what he wants to give.

One Saturday morning, standing on his front porch, apparently he decides he's had enough, and he confronts me and says, "What's the matter, Zak? I thought we had a relationship, but you're pulling away from me. From me and Robin both. I will not tolerate being treated the way you treat your mother. Either we go back to where we were, or it's over."

Really? *I think.* You're giving me an ultimatum? You dare tell me it doesn't feel good to have somebody pull away from you? You're a grown-up. You don't like it? How do you think it felt to a little kid?

"You want an answer? I'll give you one when I'm ready," I say.

A couple nights later, against my better judgment, Michelle and I honor a dinner invitation made before the falling out. I feel like it's not going to go well, but Michelle is a peacemaker and argues that we should all try to get along. For the first two hours, we do. We make small talk and eat, ignoring the proverbial "elephant in the room," and then we move to the living room. The elephant follows us.

"So, Zachary, we need to talk about something," Robin says. This is a challenge on two levels: first, that she knows I hate being called Zachary, and second, that she has decided to confront me on the issue. Her tone is nasty and condescending, while at the same time making a gesture I'm sure she thinks is magnanimous—she's putting on a show again, a public display. She has decided she is calling the shots and has authority over me, and she thinks she can intimidate me, the way she did for years. Not anymore. "I thought things were going well between you and your father."

I've had it with her, and realize I don't have to sit here and listen to her scold me.

"Are you kidding me?" I say. "You're acting like I'm supposed to owe you something. As far as I'm concerned, you were nothing but a shit to me my whole life. You were abusive to me, and you terrified me, and you knew you were doing it."

I spell out for her the things she did. She starts crying.

"Maybe I could have treated you differently," she says, "but lots of kids have been through much worse. Why can't you learn from the past and be stronger for it? Why can't you get over it?"

Get over it? Who is she to tell me to get over it? She wants me to learn from the past, as if I'd made mistakes that could teach me something. I did learn one thing from my past—I learned, when I became a Marine, to stand up for myself and hold my ground.

"You're not entitled to tell me to get over it, Robin," I say. "You're not entitled to do anything other than apologize and ask for my

forgiveness. You're completely full of shit. You might be able to fool everybody else, but you can't fool me. As long as I'm alive, I'll know what you did, and who you really are."

For the first time in my life, I see her break down. I don't feel good about it, but I don't feel bad either. There's no lasting gratification. She made me feel bad for years. If she feels bad for a few minutes, it's not like now we're even.

"It's because of both of you that I don't want to have kids," I tell her.

"Maybe I was hard on you, but I don't know what you expect me to do about it now," she says between sobs. How do I feel? I don't feel sympathetic. I'm surprised, but it's all too little and too late, and nothing she could say can undo the damage done. Her tears are meaningless.

My dad has been surprisingly quiet throughout our interaction, until now.

"Why don't you grow up and be a man?" he says to me.

In his mind, it's my job, my responsibility, to fix what went wrong in the past. He continues throwing stones.

"And what's this crap about you not wanting kids? Don't even think about using me and the way I treated you as an excuse to not want to have kids of your own."

I think, What the hell is going on here!? Who are these people? These self-centered narcissists?

I'm borderline furious, ready to turn things from verbal to physical. The sheer disrespect directed at me is too much to handle.

"You're not just a pathetic excuse for a father," I tell him. "You're a pathetic excuse for an adult."

"Right now," my father says, "you are waving a red flag at a bull."

But he has no idea which one of us is the bull. Suddenly I know that if the conversation continues, we'll fight, and if we do, I'll kill him, or at the very least, put him in the hospital. The irony is not lost on me that I am standing up to him, the way I might have stood up to all the kids who bullied me. He has indeed taught me how to be a man, by serving as a poor example of one.

"Come on," I tell Michelle, who is in tears, and I feel bad that she has had to see this. "We need to go."

Then it's two and a half years later, and I'm thirty-two, living in Southern California. My father and I haven't spoken in more than two years. It's 8:30 on a Wednesday night when the phone rings, and my caller ID tells me the call is coming from Wisconsin, but I don't recognize the number. I know it's not my father or my mother calling, so I pick up. It's my Uncle Greg. I've managed to stay reasonably close with him over the years. I sit down on the steps that lead into the living room to take the call.

"I'm afraid I have some bad news, Zak," he says. "I'm heading over to the hospital with Robin. She said your dad went unconscious at home on the living room floor and she called an ambulance. They're taking him there now. I don't know what's going to happen. I'll call you with an update."

"Keep me in the loop," I say.

I realize I should probably be more affected by the news, but I'm not. I look over at Michelle and tell her what I've just learned.

"Oh my God," she says. "Are you okay?"

"Yeah," I say, half-laughing. "I wonder what's going to happen if he dies?"

It's the first thought that comes to mind, one I've never had before. How will I feel? How will it affect the family? Will there be any regrets? My bemused tone is just false bravado, me trying to show I'm above being saddened by the loss—but what am I losing? A man who was never there? A chance to patch things up? But if we were going to patch things up, it was his turn to make the first move, not mine, and in two years, his best effort was an email blaming me for the evening at their house.

Ten minutes later, my uncle calls back. I know what he's about to say.

"Zak," he says. "Your dad is gone."

I'm not shocked or caught off guard. For some reason, I've been expecting this. I have not been expecting good news.

"So I guess by the time they got him to the hospital," my uncle continues, "he'd already—"

"It's all right," I say, cutting him off. All I can think is how he just lost a brother, and he must be devastated, but instead of addressing his own grief, he's trying to help me. He is the conduit between me and my father, even in death, and he wants things to be right between us, so he's putting his own needs aside and doing what he thinks has to be done, being strong for me. "You shouldn't be worrying about me. I'm truly grateful for the call, but you should be taking care of yourself. Just be present there. I'm okay."

After he hangs up, I tell Michelle the news. She looks at me, trying to read me to know what to say or do, but I'm not giving her much information as to my emotional state, probably because I'm not all too clear about it myself. I'm feeling very practical, or maybe numb, or maybe cold-hearted, or some combination of the three. I can't quite see how the fact that he's just died is supposed to change my feelings toward him. The facts were the facts, and they spoke for themselves. I can tell that Michelle wants answers from me, but I don't have any, so rather than stay home, unable to talk to her or answer her questions, I tell her I need to go to the gym. I kiss her goodbye, and I know she understands why I need to be alone. I tell her she should call somebody if she needs to talk, maybe even my mom.

At the gym, I do thirty minutes of circuit training, not focusing on any one thing. I felt strange, thinking, I'm the same guy I was when I was here yesterday, except now I don't have a father. *But something always happens when I work out. Something about keeping my body occupied and challenging it to perform always clears my mind. It's not that while I work out, I try consciously to think of the things I need to do or the answers to my question, but rather, when I'm working out, the answers just come to me.*

I realize my family will be coming together, physically and emotionally. They all live in the Milwaukee/Racine area and will probably be getting together at someone's house. I should be there with them. My resentment toward my father has not diminished, but it's time to put it on the shelf for a while.

As I finished my dinner at McDonald's, I briefly wished I had a gym I could go to, even though I was certain I'd be getting all the exercise I needed tomorrow. The gym is probably one of the few places on Earth where I feel at home and at ease. I remembered my father's funeral, how so many people came, a line forming outside the funeral home that went back to the street and around the corner at the end of the block, and how highly respected he was as an X-ray technician by the people who worked with him. People kept telling me how intelligent and organized he was, and I thought that if I'm intelligent or orderly, perhaps I inherited those genes from him. I wondered how many of the people at the funeral knew he'd left my mother with a sixteen-week-old baby to marry the woman he was having an affair with, but I said nothing.

The boy and his dad left. I realized eating at McDonald's and seeing the two of them had afforded me this insight—I understood why I was unable to abandon the dog. I would not do to him, or to anyone, what my father did to me. I would not become like him. I wasn't proving it to him, as if I had some sort of magical or mystical idea that he was looking down from heaven, watching me. I wasn't proving anything to myself, either, because I felt no need. It was simple. I knew what the right thing to do was, so I had to do it.

The question was, how?

On my way back to the motel, I called Michelle to fill her in since our last conversation from the general store. She heard the outrage in my voice when I told her I thought somebody had intentionally abandoned the dog. I told her how I'd left him with food and water, and how it looked like I'd be on my own, trying to get him out.

"How are you doing?" she said. "You don't sound so good."

I told her about the kittens in the sofa, and that the whole day had been enormously upsetting, a lot of emotional ups and downs.

"You're taking a lot on," she said. "You do that."

"It'll be all right."

"I'm sure it will be."

"You know me. I overthink everything."

"I know I don't have to say this," she said, "but be careful. Come home safe."

We both knew there was no talking me out of it now.

"I'll call you in the morning with the details and the drop-dead time," I told her. "Once I get out of town, there's no cell coverage."

"Okay. Love you."

"Love you. Sleep well."

"You, too. Do your best."

She meant do my best to get some sleep, because she knows how I obsess over the details when I'm planning something.

The parking lot at the Motel 6 was already filling up with semi-tractor-trailers, but the vacancy sign was still lit. I checked in and parked as close to the room as I could, hauling in all of my climbing equipment. The room was dark and stuffy, so I turned on all the lights and cranked the air conditioner to maximum. The fan was strong enough to billow out the curtains. I used the extra bed to lay out my gear.

You can't make any mistakes, I told myself. I recalled learning a certain kind of logical focus as a Marine. Once, when our platoon

45

came under "friendly fire" during a training exercise where live rounds were accidentally fired at us, I had the presence of mind to stand up and give the cease-fire sign, my arms crossed over my head, even though the lieutenant in charge told me to get down. If I'd listened to him, it might have gotten someone killed.

I found myself recalling acronyms I'd been taught as a Marine as a way to make sure nothing got overlooked. SAFESOC stood for Security, Avenues of Approach, Fields of Fire, Entrenchments, Supplementary and Alternate Positions, Obstacles and Camouflage. SMEAC stood for Situation, Mission, Execution, Admin and Logistics, Command/Signal. BAMCIS meant Begin Planning, Arrange Reconnaissance, Make Reconnaissance, Complete Planning, Issue Order, Supervise.

I worked through the process in the order of events sequentially. First, I would need to make sure my anchor was secure. I'd proven I could use my ATV as an anchor, and the dog and crate would not add substantially to the load on the line.

I was more concerned about abrasion. A tensioned line is easier to cut through than an unloaded one. As the rope passed over the edge of the canyon, it would take a near ninety-degree downward turn, making it the most likely spot for failure. I would also be on the rope longer than I was the first time I'd dropped in, and working my way back up the rope was not going to be quick or easy. The additional time meant the rope would have that much longer to abrade at the fail point. Fortunately, I'd brought an edge guard with me, an eighteen-inch-long piece of heavy fire hose that could be folded over the rope lengthwise and secured to itself with Velcro. If I could get it to stay in place at the edge of the cliff, I thought, I should be fine.

I continued going down my list. I checked my harness for wear. I clipped onto it more carabiners than I'd probably need, but I'd be bringing in and out extra gear and wanted to overcompensate.

I checked my descender. I added my heavy leather gloves, because the extra weight was going to generate extra heat, and given the length of the drop, I wanted as much protection from the heat as possible. I've seen pictures of climbers who ripped the skin off their hands because their gloves weren't equal to the task.

I added my ascending kit to the pile—the most critical piece of equipment I had. An ascender is an aluminum or steel device that locks onto the rope, with a cam inside that allows the rope to pass in one direction as you move up the rope, but prevents the rope from moving in the opposite direction. When climbing a free-hanging rope, you use two, one to hold your place while you move the other up the rope. Each ascender is attached to your harness, and to a sling your foot goes in, and then you step your way up. To someone who's never done it, it looks like you're doing most of your climbing with your legs, but it actually requires a fair amount of upper body strength. I once ascended a hundred-foot rope wearing a thirty-pound backpack and I was absolutely exhausted by the time I reached the top, mostly due to the extra load on my arms. My climb to rescue the dog would be more than twice as long, with more weight, and I had probably been in better shape then than I was now. That was why I was being as careful as I could, planning what I would take with me. Every ounce was going to count, because when you're repeating an action three or four hundred times, it can add up. Bringing something I wouldn't need would be almost as bad as forgetting something essential.

Last, I examined the dog carrier, though it was small enough that it was probably intended for cats. It was a lightweight plastic shell, held together with a few rivets, with a door at one end, held shut with a plastic handle on the top. That it was lightweight was a plus, but it seemed too fragile for the task. I couldn't hold the crate in my hand as I climbed, so my plan was to tether it to my harness and let it dangle about three feet below me. It would, I was certain, bounce against the rocks, and possibly (hopefully not) get snagged or caught and require tugging to free it.

I had the solution in my gear, and pulled out a long strip of climber's webbing, like seatbelt material, but an inch wide, and softer, with a tensile strength of about four thousand pounds. I basically wrapped the crate the way you would a Christmas package, then secured the vertical bands from slipping around the corners by knotting them with clove hitches to a piece of cord that girded the circumference. I could tie on with a carabiner where the straps intersected at the top of the package, where the bow and ribbons would go. The straps along the sides would prevent the door from accidentally opening, preventing a potentially disastrous moment.

For a tether, I would use an adjustable daisy chain, a length of webbing with a fixed loop at the end that clipped to my harness and an adjustable slide at the other, preceding a second loop I could use to clip to the crate. By adding or removing slack, I would be able to adjust the distance between myself and the crate, depending on the circumstances I found myself in. To ensure I would have as much freedom of movement as possible, I decided I would clip the tether to my harness at the rear, near the small of my back, leaving my legs free to work the ascenders or push away from the rock in front of me. Then it occurred to me that there was an overhanging ledge about a hundred feet up from the canyon floor. I had enough rope to attach a long tethering line to the crate, climb to the ledge, rest, attach a pulley to my main climbing rope with a Gibbs cam to grab the rope and serve as a dead man's brake, just in case I were somehow forced to let go, and hoist the crate to the ledge with the pulley. Working with any rope system, and in particular when you're climbing solo, in addition to double and triple-checking the mechanical elements, you have to take into account the possibility of unexpected human failure, such as a heart attack or a stroke. You have to plan for what you can't plan for. If I dropped dead, for some reason, the Gibbs cam would save the dog from a fatal plummet.

I turned off the lights and lay on the bed with my eyes closed, mentally rehearsing what I would do in the morning, visualizing each step in the process to make sure I hadn't forgotten anything. It was hard to stop thinking about it. I needed to be rested, but falling asleep was difficult. I wasn't worried about whether I'd be able to do it, because I wasn't allowing failure to be an option. I would be exhausted afterward, I thought, maybe more than I'd ever been before, but I would find a way to do it. I would summon the strength from somewhere.

But there are always surprises. The worst case scenario would be a sudden rainstorm, somewhere up-canyon in the catchment. I pictured myself in the pothole, on my knees, trying to get the dog into the crate but stopping at the sound of something growing louder, like the rumble of a train approaching, and then I'd turn to look up-canyon, where I'd see a wall of raging water about to crash down on me. I'd take a deep breath and grab hold of my rope, but the dog . . .

Or maybe the worst case scenario was something simpler, quieter. Something more likely. I would climb down into the canyon, and cross to where I left the dog, and kneel down, and put my hand on him, and feel something cold and lifeless. I would shine a light into his eyes, and maybe hold my eyeglasses in front of his nostrils to see if they fogged up, but they wouldn't, and then I would know I was too late. That I should have acted sooner, should have found a crate and brought it with me when I brought the food and water in, should have . . .

I have lived my whole life with "should have"s and "could have"s and "would have"s. If I didn't get the dog out, alive, it might be the biggest disappointment I'd ever feel, and I would have nobody to blame but myself. Michelle and everyone else would assure me that I did everything I could, but I'd know I didn't. And I obsess over my failures. Lying in bed at the Motel 6, I understood that I was setting myself up for a colossal failure. Some people fail over and over again and seem completely oblivious to it. My mother, for instance.

Oh great, I thought *Another happy thought to fall asleep to.*

I am eight years old, at home, in my room, in bed. It's 2:30 in the morning when I hear a noise and awaken to realize the lights are on. The noise I hear is my mother cursing. I am a neat child who keeps a spotless room. When I'm finished with my Lincoln Logs, I put them back in the cardboard container they came in. When I'm done with my Matchbox cars, I put them back in the display case that holds them. My closet is next to my bed, and my mother is pulling boxes out of my closet, muttering, "That damn kid never puts things away properly." Her language is more violent than that. She is removing neatly stacked boxes of my toys, only to put them right back where she found them. I close my eyes and pretend I'm still asleep. After fifteen minutes, she's done rearranging my toys and leaves the room.

This happens perhaps five more times in the next few years.

I am too young to understand what it means when she spends an hour polishing the kitchen sink until there's not a speck or watermark on it, while there's dust and grime on the bathroom shelf thick enough to write your name in. I am too young to understand why she'll scrub the kitchen stove, over and over again, while junk mail and collection notices pile up on the dining room table. Or why she'll have panic attacks and be unable to move. Or why she would tell me to lie next to her on the floor and then she'd clean my ears with metal tweezers for forty-five minutes, digging so hard it made me cry. Or why she is always so late that I know I have to get a ride from someone else's parents because if I wait for a ride from my mother, I won't get to my soccer game until the second half.

All I know is that I can't count on her. I can't talk to her. I don't want to be seen with her. I am on my own, because something is not right with her.

4

I awoke before the alarm clock rang, but I usually do when I have something important on my calendar. I dressed, checked the television for the weather report—no rain was expected— and ran down to the lobby for the continental breakfast, which is how the hospitality industry tries to make cereal and toast sound more interesting than it really is. I was thinking of food only as fuel. I wondered if the dog had managed to eat any of the food I'd left him. I needed fuel to power my muscles, though in truth, I knew I could probably get down and up without eating anything, just on adrenaline. The dog needed fuel like a car with a tank so empty it was running on fumes. I saw the food I'd left him in terms of hours, or minutes. One bite would give him fifteen more minutes of life.

In my room, I checked my gear one more time and then packed up. It only then occurred to me that I didn't have much of a plan beyond getting the dog out of the canyon. If I was staying in Page another night, I might want to keep the room, but I didn't know if I was staying. My plan was only to get the dog to the animal hospital. Beyond that, I might want to explore a few other canyons I'd had my eye on.

At the same time, a kind of oppressive feeling had come over me, something I'd never felt before. I tried, at first, not to think about it, but it was hard to shake. It was something more than the occasional global pessimism I'd experienced from time to time. I had a new responsibility. A life was in my hands. As I carried my gear down to my truck, I felt a sense of purpose, a new meaning to the day, if not to my life, and I felt myself rising to the challenge in a way that quickened my step, but . . . I also felt the weight of something dark and heavy pressing me down. It wasn't fear of failure, but more a kind of gloom when I thought about the dog and, more to the point, how he got there. My task was to undo a single wrong, but it was just one wrong, one little dog in a world full of dogs and canyons and people who derived pleasure from abusing those who were weaker than them. Maybe it was that my belief in justice had been shaken, because I knew I'd never know who'd put the dog in the hole—unless the dog had a subcutaneous chip that might let the vet identify the owner, a modern improvement on the traditional collar-tagging system. But I highly doubted the dog had been chipped; it just didn't seem likely.

While I was still close to town and had cell-phone reception, I called Michelle.

"I'm heading out," I told her. "If you don't hear from me by six o'clock tonight, you can call the police and tell them where I am. I should be out way before that."

"Be careful," she said. "Do you have everything you need?"

"You didn't seriously just ask me that, did you?"

"You're right," she said. "I'm sure you were up half the night, planning everything."

"Not quite half the night," I said.

"I'm sure everything is going to be okay and that you've thought of everything, but I'm going to say it anyway—be careful. You have to take care of yourself just as much as you have to take care of the dog."

"I will," I said.

"Anything I can do from here?" she asked.

"Yeah," I said. "You can call the Page Animal Hospital and tell them I'll be bringing in a malnourished puppy. I'm hoping I can be there around noon."

"I will," she said. "Love you."

"Love you."

I drove for an hour on a washboard gravel road, blasting the soundtrack from the movie *Gladiator* on the CD player in my truck to cut above the rumble and distract me from the anxiety I felt. It felt like the drive was taking forever, my agony accentuated by the corrugated road surface, but I found that if I sped up and took the road between fifty-five and sixty miles per hour, the jarring and the noise lessened.

According to what I knew about the biology of starvation, time was of the essence. Starvation works something like this: If you can compare a human (or a canine) body to a locomotive, it's a machine that has to keep burning fuel to move forward and continue to exist. Normally, we eat food, it enters our stomachs, and it breaks down into various elements. Carbohydrates become blood glucose, which the muscles convert to glycogen for energy. The reason there's a national obesity epidemic has much to do with how we evolved during an ancient time when we had to go long periods between feasting on wooly mammoths: we'd evolved to burn the things that gave the most energy first—sugars and proteins—and store the heavier fuels, meaning fat, for later. We evolved to endure a cycle of feasts and famines, but now, for most of us, we eat foods high in sugars, burn that, and store the fats for the famine that never comes. If there's no new ingestion of food as fuel, the body consumes the fuel in the stomach in about twenty-four hours and then starts burning up fat reserves (lipolysis). When there's no fat left to burn, the body starts burning muscle and organ tissue for fuel (proteolysis) to keep the engine going and the onboard computer, the brain and central nervous system, functioning to prevent everything from falling apart. Car by car, the train starts to consume itself.

The body also needs food for more than just raw fuel. It needs the vitamins and minerals in food to fight off diseases and maintain a chemical balance. Without them, victims of starvation come down with diseases such as scurvy, pellagra, beriberi, or anemia, which can lead ultimately to edema and heart failure. In a weakened state, the body becomes vulnerable to all kinds of diseases, bacterial or fungal infections, that it would otherwise be able to fight off. The brain needs energy to keep functioning, and when the brain runs out of gas, there can be permanent brain damage. Eventually, the train burns itself up and the locomotive grinds to a halt.

At my former campsite, I found a flat spot to park and unloaded my ATV. I drank as much water as I could, because I'd be working in the hot sun. I planned to bring only a single water bottle down the rope with me so that I'd be carrying as little weight as possible. With my gear strapped to both the front and rear cargo racks of the Grizzly, I paused for a second before pressing the starter.

I listened.

I would say I was listening to the sound of the desert, but the desert doesn't make a sound. Even on a windy day, you might hear the wind pushing past your ears, but there are no trees that sway in the breeze and no leaves that rustle against each other. Even when there are birds, it seems as though they keep their voices down, rather than give away their locations. Some people like to go to busy restaurants or sit in the food court at a shopping mall and lose themselves in the white noise and the din of human community and commerce, but I've never been one of them. For me, my soul stops circling and comes to rest and I find the calm, still center of myself in a place like this—the open empty silent desert.

When I say I paused to listen, I mean I paused to *not* listen, to hear nothing, to breathe the cool morning air and set myself. Against the backdrop of silence, the danger and the risk of what I was going to do stood out and moved to the foreground, but simultaneously became clearer and more manageable. I subtracted from my thoughts anything that didn't address the task before me and took a deep breath before starting the ATV and heading for the drop in, skirting small boulders and following the tracks I'd left in the sand the day before, still visible in the slanting morning light.

From the surface, slot canyons are virtually invisible. You can't see them, gazing at the horizon, and because they're so narrow, if you're crossing the desert on an ATV at high speed, you could drive right into one before you're able to stop. In the open desert, there aren't any warning signs to tell you where they are. That was why I decided to start from my original campsite, and why, even following my own tracks, I could only run at half throttle.

Then I reached the rim. It was perhaps fifty to sixty yards across the chasm. Looking down, I remembered a rappel I once did off a piece of rock in Yosemite Valley called Taft Point, one of the higher ledges in a valley known for its multi-thousand-foot cliff walls. For some reason I can't recall, I thought, mistakenly, that it would be amusing to hang suspended above a bottomless void, a two-thousand-foot emptiness below me. I tied off to a massive rock at the top and went over the edge, partly to test my own level of confidence. It's hard to explain, but when you're two-thousand feet above the ground but you still have contact with the rock and your feet are connected to the earth, the height doesn't bother you. When you're dangling above the ground like a yo-yo at the bottom of a string, however, it's disorienting and intolerable, even though the depth of the crater you're going to make if you hit the ground, or the square footage of the splat if you land on flat rock, are the same.

In Yosemite, I lowered myself about fifteen feet into the void, with another hundred feet of rope below me, and then I changed my mind because in no time, I started spinning and my muscle groups started clenching in ways they weren't meant to clench, and my palms started sweating inside my gloves, and I was gripping the rope with my braking hand so hard my hand started to cramp. Even experienced climbers can get vertigo, because when you're at the end of a rope spinning in space, you don't have a frame of reference, and it feels like the world is spinning, a big disk on a turntable beneath you, and there's nothing you can do to arrest your motion. It took considerable concentration just to loosen my grip. I tied off and started rigging my ascender kit, but between the adrenaline and the fear (assuming those were two different things) and spinning in space, it was monumentally difficult to function, physically or mentally, and it felt like it took an hour to secure my foot loops and clip on my ascenders.

Yosemite had humbled me. The slot canyon in front of me presented a similar opportunity for failure, even though I'd done it successfully the day before. The term Navy and Air Force aviators used in Tom Wolfe's book *The Right Stuff* was "screw the pooch," meaning "mess up royally," although "mess" isn't the word most people use. In my case, "screwing the pooch" had taken on a slightly more literal meaning. I remembered that there was a dog down there, and I'd made a promise to it that I'd be back to save it, and, to me, it made no difference that it was a dog that didn't understand English. A promise is a promise is a promise. Maybe he didn't, but I understood English just fine.

I used the ATV as an anchor, as I had the day before, chocking the wheels with stones and tying the hand brakes with cords, anchoring my rappel line to the rear hitch and tying a redundant hitch to the front bumper. I joined my two longest lengths of rope together, 465 feet combined (that's a bit more than one and a half football fields), with a figure-eight knot and made sure I hadn't somehow inadvertently tied a knot I didn't need in the middle of one of my lines. I glanced one last time to the west, where any bad weather was likely to come from, but the sky was a cloudless blue. I set my camera up on my ATV to make a video of myself as I threw my line over the edge and into the canyon. When I watch this video, I can count off almost twenty seconds before I see the camera suddenly shake, indicating that the line had jerked taut as it reached the end.

I gulped involuntarily.

I wrapped the heavy canvas edge guard around my line and then donned and attached my harness rig, which I'd set up the night before, clipping on in front of the edge guard, which I would slide down the rope behind me to make sure it positioned properly. The last thing I did, before putting on my climbing gloves, was don my backpack containing the rest of my gear with the dog crate clipped to the backpack where it would be out of the way.

I began my descent, walking backward down a slope that got steeper and steeper until, perhaps thirty or forty feet from my ATV, I reached the place where my line angled sharply down. I set my edge guard and was thankful I had it.

I fed line through my figure eight slowly and worked methodically, careful not to overheat my line or my braking glove. At the ledge, halfway down, I paused to gather my thoughts and again, as I had the day before, passed my joining knot through my figure eight. Before continuing my descent, I remembered to take up the slack above me. A rope with a lot of stretch is called "dynamic," and a rope with no or little stretch is called "static." I was using a static rope, but I still had over 150 feet above me that I'd released from gravity when I stopped on the ledge, which meant it had considerable slack in it. An inexperienced climber can forget about that slack, resume a descent, and take a very sudden and unexpected, if brief, plunge.

I was grateful that I was not an inexperienced climber, and then something odd occurred to me. It was an idea I hadn't quite been able to put my finger on before, but it seemed as if everything in my life had both led me to this point and prepared me for it. It seemed strange and grandiose to consider, but it felt like I was meant to do this, and that nobody else would have responded to the situation the way I did. Nobody else would have been as prepared or as ready, because somehow, now, all my suffering had a meaning, or a purpose. I was fighting back, even though the demons I was battling were years behind me.

It's seventh grade, still early in the school year, but I now know that nothing is going to change, certainly not for the better, and probably for the worse. But I've been carrying this weight with me for a long time all by myself, without talking to anybody about it. That is often what bullied kids do. They feel completely embarrassed to admit what's happening to them. One day, feeling like nothing is going to change, I make the mistake of telling my mother how I'm being picked on. It has occurred to me that she should have noticed by now that something is wrong, but she has never been that attentive or engaged.

Her response is to make me feel like it's my fault.

"Why do they pick on you?" she asks me. "Why don't you just make friends?"

Gosh, *I think.* Why didn't I think of that?

To her credit, rather than ignore it, she feels she has to do something about it, but it feels like it's mostly because of how it looks to the neighbors. She decides to walk me to school one day, which only adds a new layer of humiliation. As I feared it would, now in addition to being pathetic and an easy target, I am also seen as a baby who has gone crying to his mommy.

Being bullied devalues you as a person in a subtle but pernicious way, because not only do other people identify you as an easy target, but you start to identify yourself as such. My mother's reaction to the news makes me feel like she's disappointed in me. As we walk to school, all I can think is that I am that kid, the one no parent wants. We go in the back door to avoid the mass of kids hanging out front before school. We meet with the principal, and as expected, nothing of significance happens. I hear a few platitudes about how my teachers will be told to be more vigilant. (The truth is, faculty members are seldom in a position to help a bullied child.) Bullies are smart enough to know when and where to pick on their targets. Bullies are adept at knowing how not to get caught. This is simply my reality. This is why I don't bother talking to adults about my situation.

After that, when my mother asks me how things are going, I lie and say everything is okay because I am hoping to salvage what little pride I have left.

Only once does a teacher notice anything is wrong. I'm coming back from lunch one day when my homeroom teacher sees me and asks me what was going on. Mrs. Kulba is, in a way, the quintessential junior high school teacher, with horn-rimmed eyeglasses and colorful sweaters, in her late fifties and a bit heavy, with an unshakably even temperament, the kind that only comes from years of dealing with kids. I tell her I'm getting picked on, and that it's bad, and that I'm afraid. She tells me a story she thinks will cheer me up.

"It's about a girl I knew. She can laugh about it now," my homeroom teacher confides, "but a few years ago, there was a girl who was being picked on by some of the other girls, and she fought back pretty hard and actually hurt one of the girls who was picking on her. And

the teachers saw it, but somehow, when we were asked, none of us
remembered what we saw, if you know what I mean."

(*But telling a scared kid "fight back" is a meaningless thing to say.*) !
What she's saying is, "I'm not going to help you—you're on your own."
All I can think is that fighting is dangerous. Confrontation is the last
thing I want. I think, "Why should I have to fight? Why should I have
to? Other kids didn't have to—why should I? Why me?"

My feet hit the ground with a thud. I could feel the air getting
cooler and cooler the deeper I went, and here at the bottom in
the early morning, the temperature was at least ten degrees lower
than at the top. As I unclipped from my rope, I was once again
overcome by the fear that I was too late and the dog had died in
the night. The concept of "fighting back" took on a new meaning,
because now it meant fighting against time or fighting to simply
survive another day—fighting the urge to just give up.

I didn't exactly tiptoe to the lip of the pothole, but I moved
furtively, as though I could lessen the impact of any potential
bad news by sneaking up on it. As I descended, I realized the
coolness might have been a good thing. In the winter, the dog
at the bottom of the hole might have frozen to death, but in
the summer, an animal exposed to the hot sun in the heat of
day without food or water would not have lasted long. Too hot
would have been as bad as too cold, but here, three hundred feet
below the surface in June, conditions for survival were almost
optimal. When I peeked over the lip of the pothole, I saw the
black shape of the dog on the blue towel, where I'd left him,
but it appeared that the food and water I'd left him had been
partially consumed, and none of the small Styrofoam bowls had
been knocked over.

I whistled.

Nothing.

"Hey," I said in a voice loud enough to be heard but soft enough not to startle. I watched, waiting for a response. This wasn't good.

Then I saw one of his ears twitch.

Now it was a race against time, but I had to maintain situational awareness, when a mistake could still be fatal to both of us. I reset a hand line to take me down into the hole, using the same bolt I'd rigged yesterday, before donning my backpack, the crate still attached, and then I lowered myself into the pothole. I took my backpack off when I reached the bottom and knelt beside the dog.

"Hey buddy," I said as I laid my hand on his side. "I told you I'd be back."

He didn't open his eyes, but I could feel his lungs expanding, just barely, as he breathed. I thought of those scenes in the movies where someone is hurt and some doctor says, "It's too dangerous to move him." The dog and I didn't have a choice.

Closer now, I could see that he'd managed to eat more of the vile canned goop I'd left for him, and he'd drunk some of the water. I couldn't see any vomit on the ground beside him, so I assumed he'd kept down whatever he'd eaten. The ember of life inside him was still glowing, if only faintly.

"We'll get you some more food and water once we get you out of here," I said, picking up the bowls and placing them in a trash bag I'd brought with me.

I moved the crate next to him and opened the door, and then puzzled for a moment as to the best way to get him into it. I'd already prepared the crate to cushion the ride with a few extra towels the cleaning lady at the Page Animal Hospital provided me, but the dog looked like he might break in half if I lifted him the wrong way. I worked my fingers gently under the towel he was lying on and, in one steady slow motion, raised him a few inches from the ground. It was like lifting a pile of soap bubbles. I slid him three quarters of the way into the crate, tail first, set him down, and then tugged on the lead corners of the towel to slide him in the rest of the way. He hadn't so much as flinched or even blinked, but he was still breathing. Maybe he was asleep, I thought, dreaming of whatever happy place he'd come from, though I wondered if it was possible that he'd been abused from the day he was born. I hoped that if he died during his ride up out of the canyon, or on the road headed back to Page, he might somehow leave this world knowing that it wasn't all bad and that someone had cared about him.

"We'll be out of here in no time," I told him as I adjusted the towels around him to keep him from rolling into the sides of the crate when it banged against the rocks, as it inevitably would.

I closed the latch and retied the webbing and climbing cord around the package, double-checking everything to make sure nothing had shifted and that all my knots and hitches were secure. I tied a hundred-foot length of cord to the webbing at the top of the crate and clipped the other end to my harness, before I walked myself up the chute and out of the pothole using the hand line, pausing for just a moment first to take it all in.

As much as I remained concerned and worried that the dog still might not make it, I felt something else happening now inside of me—a sense of pride, perhaps. I knew I was doing something I could be proud of myself for, which is always an ego booster. But more than that, I felt an odd sense of gratitude, though I couldn't say to whom I was grateful. In ancient times, I might have been grateful to the gods or maybe the Fates, thinking some supernatural force had brought me here. I don't believe in supernatural forces, but I was glad, all the same, to think I'd been given this opportunity—that I knew what I was doing, that I was young and strong enough to do this, and that I was altering this poor animal's destiny, intervening in its fate. We probably all alter each other's destinies a hundred times a day without knowing it, but this time, I knew it.

"Time to get you out of here," I said.

At the top of the chute, I turned to hoist the crate hand over hand, leaning out as far as I dared and fully extending my arms to raise the crate up vertically, rather than drag it up the slope. I wanted to lift him at a slow, steady rate. In no time, the crate felt like it gained ten pounds every time I switched hands to hoist him up. Two feet off the ground, the crate banged against the rock, and I cursed, because that was exactly what I was trying to avoid. I leaned out even further, and for a second almost lost my balance and felt myself slowly tipping forward, about to dive headfirst fifteen feet down, which might not sound like much, but it was still enough to kill me. I threw my head back and then braced my right knee against the canyon wall to stabilize. I was more secure, but the crate banged against the rock again, and I became angrier and angrier at myself for allowing it to do so. But . . . the anger helped me. It pushed me forward. When the crate was five feet off the ground, I rotated to my left and swung the crate into the chute, which let me bring my arms in closer to my body. My arms and shoulders were burning, but then, suddenly, the crate was out of the pothole, and I was able to set the crate down in the sandy wash and rest, out of breath.

"Let's hope that was the hardest part," I said, looking into the crate. The dog was either asleep or unconscious. "Oh, really? I'm saving your life and you're going to sleep through the whole thing?"

But I knew that his state at that moment was better than if he were awake and panicking. I paused for a minute and shot a brief video of him, as if I could show it to him later. As much as I like being alone, this was something I wanted to share with someone. The puppy was out, asleep, or else he'd simply resigned himself to whatever it was I was doing with him.

I waited another moment or two for my arms to recover—even in my most brutal workouts at the gym, lifting weights straight up with my arms fully extended was not something I'd ever done— and then I moved to my rappel line to rig my ascenders. I moved the crate to a position directly below my rappel line, which also served as a plumb bob marking the spot directly beneath the upper anchor; it wouldn't do to lift the crate from the canyon floor and have it start to swing from side to side as a pendulum. I double-checked the webbing around the crate, and the knot I'd used to tie on the tether, and then I double-checked my own gear and my climbing harness. One word that might be used to describe my mindset is "fastidious." Another might be "obsessive" or maybe even "maniacal," but to me it was just what I've always done, planning ways to be safe, paying attention to all the details and troubleshooting what could go wrong—the same mindset I had when I was waiting for the bus, or entering the school cafeteria, asking myself, "Where are the threats located? What's most likely to go wrong? What will I do if X happens, or Y, or Z?"

When I was satisfied that I'd thought of everything, twice, I began my ascent, stepping into my loops and pulling the straps tight to lock them around my foot like stirrups, then raising my left hand and left leg first in a movement that must be coordinated but is slightly counterintuitive, since when we walk, or run, we usually swing our right arm while stepping with the left foot.

I left the crate on the canyon floor and climbed quickly to the ledge approximately one hundred feet up, glad that I'd thought of the pulley system the night before when I was lying in bed, trying to fall asleep. I used two short pieces of webbing to set friction knots on my rappel line, above my ascenders, then used carabiners to set my pulley and, below that, the Gibbs cam, and then I untied the tether from behind my back and fed the line through the cam and the pulley. Now I could pull down on the line to raise the crate, and if I were to let go for some reason, the Gibbs cam would serve as an emergency brake.

I raised the crate in a slow but steady motion, until, no worse for wear, I had the dog at my feet. I picked the crate up and walked up the slope to where the ledge met the wall. When I tried to look in the crate, I couldn't get a good look at the dog because of all the towels I'd packed in to keep him from sliding or rolling around inside the crate. This was no place to untie the package to check on him, so all I could do was cross my fingers and hope he was okay.

I undid my pulley system and packed it away, then retethered the crate to my harness using the adjustable daisy chain, leaving enough length that I wouldn't kick the crate each time I took a step. Matching adjustable daisy chains attached my harness to the upper grips of my ascenders, which would allow me, if I got tired during the climb, to take my hands off the grips and "sit" in my harness to rest.

"Now comes the fun part," I said to the dog, once I was rested, but I sensed my ironic tone was lost on him.

With the crate tethered to hang about three feet below me, I returned to my rappel line, leaned back to absorb the slack, and took three steps up. When I tested the crate, it seemed relatively light. I would be free-hanging for the next 125 feet or so, in some places as close as eight inches from the rock face, but still too far off it to use my feet for purchase or relief.

I started up and soon realized I was going to need to change my approach; usually I climb in large powerful steps, and the fewer of them the better, but now when I did, the crate below me swung wildly with each step, and worse—I was still close enough to the rock that when the crate swung, it banged off the wall. I found I had to take short baby steps and push away from the rope with my arms to keep the crate, which was going to sway no matter what

I did, from banging. I've never taken a yoga class, but I'm sure there's some sort of yoga exercise that involves holding your arms out in front of you for as long as you can, and then holding them out longer, and then holding them out until you feel like they're going to spontaneously combust. I was doing that, but I was also lifting weights with both my arms and legs.

Fifty feet above the ledge, I bonked. I couldn't push any farther. I let go of my ascenders and sat back in the harness, spent and out of breath, my arms screaming with pain, my shoulders hot and knotted. The air here was warmer, and I was working in sunlight, leaving me drenched in sweat. I'd drunk my entire water bottle at the bottom, to lose the weight, which might sound like it doesn't make sense because the weight would be inside of me instead of in my backpack, but the backpack was making me top heavy and adding to the strain on my arms. By now I'd probably sweated off more water than I'd taken in anyway.

I didn't feel fully recovered, but I remembered I was racing the clock. The idea that I might leave the canyon floor with a live dog but reach the top with a dead one was too much to consider, so I started up again, less concerned now with jostling the dog and focused more on just making it out of the hole, which was now, as I neared the top, wide and gaping. When I glanced down, the two canyon walls converged to create a sort of false vanishing point, an illusion of distance supplemented by the lack of any frame of reference to confer scale. For a brief moment, I felt like I was a mile high.

Perhaps seventy-five feet above the ledge below and the same distance from the top, I bonked again. My legs were okay, but my arms and shoulders were aflame with pain, and despite the generous padding, my harness was biting into my waist. It was like sitting on a sling made out of piano wire rather than three-inch-wide nylon webbing. The crate, which seemed so manageable at first, felt like it weighed five hundred pounds. I needed help, but help was nowhere to be found. My cell phone was in my backpack, but being below the rim of the canyon meant I had no reception. I'd worked out for years in weight rooms, so I'd been here before—that point where you think you want to just call it a day, a bad day, and try again tomorrow.

In fact, I'd been to that point before I ever started working out in weight rooms.

It's seventh grade. Two days before Christmas, I'm walking to school and I find myself passing a row of cars where a group of older kids, the ones popularly dubbed "The Burnouts," are parked. I assume my nemesis Ben is among them. I'd say chief nemesis, but on any given day, it feels like the rankings change, and it's hard to keep track.

When I realize where I am, alarms go off. I should know better than to walk past The Burnouts, but I'm in a hurry. I've been careless. I've let my guard down. Usually if I know they're there, I'll make a detour. They generally sit inside their cars before the bell rings, smoking cigarettes and listening to heavy metal music, bobbing their heads, either stoned already or getting there. Most of them are older than me, and even the ones who are my age seem older somehow. I'm not small of stature, but inside, I am in many ways still a little kid, and these schoolmates seem like grown-ups, and hostile ones at that. They know things I will never know, and they've done things I will never do. They are bad enough, taken individually, but when they gather in groups, they take strength from each other and dare or goad each other on.

When I realize what I'm walking into, I have about three seconds to decide whether to reverse course, which will make me look like a coward and invite being abused as such, or keep walking with my head down and hope they're too busy doing whatever it is Burnouts do to notice me.

I keep walking, trying not to attract attention. In my head, I'm screaming at myself, saying, "Stupid stupid stupid—why weren't you paying attention?"

For a while, I think I've almost made it. I'd walk faster, but I don't want to create the appearance that I'm running. I don't want to look like I'm afraid, which in a way doesn't make sense since I'm pretty sure they all know I'm afraid.

I reach the last of the Burnout cars, staring straight ahead to avoid eye contact. As I near the last car, the car door opens and a short blonde girl wearing blue jeans and a scruffy jean jacket gets out with a cigarette in her hand. Her name is Leona. She's skinny—a lot of the girls in the Burnout crowd are skinny from doing drugs—and she is wearing too much eye makeup. She is two years older than me. She has no reason to know who I am, except as "that kid who nobody likes." Behind her is a kid in my grade named Jerry, her boyfriend, who I know for a fact doesn't like me, though, again, I can't say why. He picks on me constantly. He must have said something to her about me in the car. Something like, "There's the kid I pick on, Leona—why don't you give it a try? It's really fun."

"Hey!" I hear her call out. "Hey—don't walk away from me when I'm talking to you."

I keep walking.

"Hey, you little shit," she says. "So you don't like people who smoke. You think smokers have a problem? Jerry says you don't like smokers."

It's nothing I actually said, only an excuse to attack me, as if they need an excuse.

Leona strides up to me aggressively. My first thought is that she's mistaken me for someone else, because I've never said anything about her to anyone—who would I say it to when no one talks to me?

Suddenly, she begins to slap me and pull my hair. I am overcome with fear. This is exactly the scenario I've lost sleep over and made myself sick over, but I'm in shock all the same at the sheer senselessness of it, the utter confusion of it. Someone I've never spoken to, never met and don't know, who doesn't know me, has decided to attack me. All my nightmares are coming true.

I fall to the ground, covering my head with my arms and rolling up into a ball, taking the blows. The girl is absolutely enraged, screaming at the top of her voice about what a "f—ing little shit" I am. She's self-righteous and entitled, as if I've wronged her in some terrible way and deserve all her abuse. I can hear her screaming. I can hear myself crying, and I can hear Jerry and the others cheering her on, but I don't understand anything. It's the most terrifying thing I've ever experienced, and it goes on and on and on. . . .

Then the bell rings. Jerry pulls her off me. I look up to see them all heading into the building.

I stay down as long as I can, letting them get as far away as possible before picking myself up, still sobbing, my face wet. I need to get to homeroom. I lower my head, embarrassed, and walk toward the school, only to raise my eyes and see the girl coming at me again. I turn away and again cover my head with my arms. I'm not sure how long the second attack lasts, but it's the same basic moves, slapping, hair pulling, probably kicking, I don't know.

Finally, she's finished. I stay where I am until they're gone. The fear I'm experiencing is greater and more intense than anything I've ever known, almost beyond description.

Angry, I decided the fatigue I felt was mental, or if it wasn't, the solution was. I don't know if adrenaline is something anybody can consciously summon, but I'd learned that determination is something anybody can draw upon. I wasn't going to fail, so I started up again, grunting and shouting at myself with each step I took, not cursing because I was frustrated or tired, but to cheer myself on.

Maybe a minute and a half later, I'd put the last of the sheer vertical behind me. I had another hundred feet up an angled wall, but I could use my feet. The problem now was that I was dragging the crate up the wall, but even walking with an exaggerated bow-legged duck-walk, I still kicked it a few times.

The cushioning worked, and the straps held, and then I was back at my ATV, where I unclipped the crate from my harness and collapsed next to my ATV. I chugged a bottle of water and then moved the crate out of the shadow of the ATV and into the sun, thinking the dog probably hasn't seen sunlight in who knew how long—maybe the warmth or the bright light burning red through his closed eyelids might have some sort of regenerative effect on him. It did on me. I felt a sense of accomplishment, but more than that, I felt a sense of triumph. We were 350 feet above the pothole and, for the dog, 350 feet above certain death. I was tired, but I felt an energy I'd never experienced before. I felt a qualified joy, knowing I'd gotten the dog this far, but mindful that although we were out of the hole, we weren't out of the woods.

It took me fifteen minutes to haul up my rope and pack away all my gear, and another fifteen to drive the ATV with one hand and steady the crate with the other to get back to my truck, where I found I had enough reception on my cell phone to send a text. I sent it to Michelle, saying simply, "We're out."

And I knew, because Michelle is someone I can count on and trust, that she would call the animal hospital and tell them to be ready for us.

The wind had picked up, and in a half dozen places, shallow sand dunes had blown across the road, but I kept the truck in four-wheel drive because nothing was going to stop us now. Driving back to Page, exhilaration gave way to fatigue, and fatigue reminded me of depression, and I started to think again of that day in seventh grade.

The day Leona attacked me was a Monday. That Wednesday is the last day before Christmas break. All morning after the attack, I'm too distraught to pay attention in any of my classes. Other schoolmates laugh at me and mock me, word quickly spreading as to what happened in the parking lot before school.

"He got his ass kicked by a girl."

"Hey Zak—I heard you got bitch-slapped."

When Jerry says, between morning classes, "Leona beat the piss out of you," I try to dismiss it and say she hadn't hurt me.

"Are you trying to dis my girlfriend?" he says. He tells me that, at lunch, he's going to really beat the shit out of me, to show me what it feels like. At lunch, I know I have to get away from school as fast as I can. Just as he said he would, Jerry tries to chase me down as soon as I step foot out the door. I run, crying, and make it to my front door. I don't go back to class that afternoon.

The next morning, I lie in bed, and I can't think of how to go forward. My life was barely manageable before, but now the fragile system of coping I'd had in place has crumbled. It's like I can't think of how to get out of bed.

I tell my mom I'm sick, which in a way is almost true—my gut is so twisted, my heart so broken, my psyche so damaged that I want to throw up and can hardly move. My pain is obvious, and I am a terrible liar, but my mother is nevertheless too oblivious to notice anything is wrong. It's not that I expect her to be a mind reader, but it seems absolutely clear that she doesn't care, or can't be bothered, and I know that even if I spell it out for her, nothing will be gained. If she walks me to school again, it will only get worse. She tells me if I'm sick I should stay home, though she has to go to work, so I'm alone all day, which is fine with me.

For the first half of that Christmas break, I stay in my house, since the girl who attacked me lives down the street, and I can see her and her friends occasionally gathering outside her house. The first half of the vacation, my anxiety levels decrease. The second half of the vacation, I feel my dread increasing daily as the vacation draws to an end, a knot in my stomach getting tighter and tighter.

When school starts again, I synchronize my watch with the school bells and time it so that if I wait thirty seconds after the first bell, I can run as fast as I can from home and make it to school about forty-five seconds before the second bell, thus avoiding running into anybody outside of school. My first day back, in gym class, Ben sees me and his face lights up with excitement as he says, "You are screwed—we've been waiting for you."

I adopt new strategies. During lunch, I avoid people by hiding in the music room and practicing my cello. The music teacher admires my dedication. I take a different route each day to get between classes to avoid certain kids. Some days, if my last class and my next class are both on the first floor, I'll go all the way up to the third floor and then walk around and down again to avoid running into Ben, Jerry, Leona, Wade, or any number of people. I'll go to the music room after school and practice the cello as an excuse to hide until everybody who can hurt me has gone home. I am, consequently, getting pretty good on the cello.

My home is my sanctuary, but only as a place to hide—not as a place to solve my problems. I wake up from tension and stress every morning at about 5:00, and then lie in bed for two and a half hours, thinking about what can happen, what can go wrong, how to stay safe. Fridays after school, I'll breathe a sigh of relief, and Saturdays are okay, but Sundays, the terror starts to build again. I'll go to church alone on Sunday morning—my mother isn't interested—and sometimes I pray for God to help me, but by Sunday afternoon, I know I'm on my own again. Sunday evenings, I have a routine where I'll watch three different outdoorsman TV shows, first Babe Winkleman's Good Fishing, *and then a fishing show hosted by a guy named Bill Dance, and a show called* The In-Fisherman, *which is over at nine, and then*

I go to bed. Fishing is a passion of mine, and watching fishing shows is a way to take my mind off my fears.

I make it through, one day at a time, but the weight never leaves me. No optimism returns. These bleak midwinter months, Lake Michigan and the sky both turn gray and stay that way for weeks at a time. The snow turns to a murky slush, everything gets grimy and dead looking, and I start to think I have no hope, no realistic way to end this daily cycle of debilitating fear and anxiety except to kill myself.

It doesn't seem like a desperate idea, just a logical, practical one. We don't have any guns in the house, but it isn't hard to think of high places I could jump from, or medications I could overdose on. What stops me is only a sense that I don't have the permission I need to make a decision like that. I lack the autonomy I would require to commit suicide. I don't worry about what my mom would think if I kill myself, because I don't care, but I am somewhat concerned about what my dad will think, because I fear him, and I know that Gary, our neighbor/landlord, who's a great guy and almost a surrogate father, will be hurt if I do anything to myself.

And as always, my mother, who should be there for me, simply is not. When she's not at work, she lies on the couch, eating Oreos and drinking Pepsi Free, disengaged from the world around her, and from me. Weekends, she spends an hour a day scrubbing every speck of dirt from the top of the stove or cleaning the sink. Does she somehow believe this is helping? There is a metaphor about the foolishness of "rearranging the deck chairs on the Titanic, *" But that's what she's doing. She is not just rearranging them. She is naming them, alphabetizing them, sterilizing them. Everything she does is irrelevant, and nothing offers any hope of changing the path I'm on, the path I travel, absolutely alone. The ship of me has hit the iceberg (or maybe the iceberg hit me), and it's going down, but unlike the* Titanic, *nobody is hearing my distress signals.*

Driving to the animal hospital, it's clear to me why I feel safe when I'm alone in nature, exploring places far away from human traffic, and why I took it so hard, so personally, when I found the dog in the canyon: Someone had violated my personal sanctuary. More to the point, I have always empathized with victims and underdogs. In this case, quite literally. There should be a patron saint for underdogs and orphans and Charlie Brown Christmas trees. St. Jude is the patron saint of desperate cases and lost causes, but only the first half of that applies, and what kind of a saint is he, anyway, if he gives up?

As I got closer to Page and had cell coverage, I called Michelle. The animal hospital would be ready for him.

"I got your text. Are you alright?" she asked.

"I'm good. Everything went pretty much as planned," I told her, glad to hear her voice and glad to share my day with her. "He hasn't really moved from when I put him in the crate, so I hope things are going to be alright. Did you contact the vet and tell them we're coming?"

"I did. They're expecting you guys shortly."

"Thanks," I said. "I really appreciate your help with this. I'm hoping this wasn't all for nothing."

"Call me once you know something."

"I will."

Michelle understood the frame of mind I was in and that I didn't want to stay on the phone and chat.

I walked into the vet's with the crate under my arm. I hadn't had a chance to shower or clean up, and I'm sure my appearance left something to be desired, but I wasn't concerned with first impressions.

"Can I help you?" the receptionist said, an older woman dressed in scrubs.

"I'm Zak Anderegg," I said. She showed no sign that she recognized my name. "I believe my wife called and told you I'd be coming."

"When would she have called?" She must have correctly interpreted the look of annoyance on my face. I wasn't expecting a team of doctors to rush out to meet me in the parking lot with a stretcher . . . or maybe I was. I was definitely not in the mood to deal with people who weren't up to speed or ready to act.

"Have a seat and I'll go check," the woman said.

I was wrong to question her competence. A woman came out of the back and told me her name was Krista and that she was the one who took the call. She looked at me, and then at the crate, and she knew what my story was. She was in her thirties and pretty, with light brown hair, and she was, like the receptionist, wearing light blue hospital scrubs.

"Let's get him out of there," she said, gesturing for me to follow her. The examination room was small and windowless, with a stainless steel table that folded out from the wall, a small sink, a chair, a stool, and a cabinet containing medical supplies. I set the crate on the table.

"Would you take the webbing off, please?" she asked me. I found tremendous relief in the idea of transferring the burden to someone else, and there was something about the way she moved and spoke that inspired confidence. Rather than waste time with knots, I used my pocket knife to slice through the cords and straps. She opened the door to the crate and looked in, and then she called for another technician to help her. They used screwdrivers to remove the top half of the crate.

"Where in the world did you find him?" she asked.

"In a deep canyon, about forty-five minutes from here. I have no idea how he got there or how long he was stuck."

She looked at me, surprised. Abandoned puppies and kittens found on the side of the road were not uncommon. Finding a puppy deep in a slot canyon was more than a little unusual.

In the veterinarian's office, with bright fluorescent lights overhead, I got my first good look at the dog, and my heart sank. His lips and gums had receded from his teeth, due, Krista told me, to dehydration. His teeth had turned a frightening dark brown. Rather than the distended belly you sometimes see when humans are starving, I saw the absence of any belly or gut, just a sucked in cavity, as if all his internal organs had withered away. For the first time, I realized he smelled terrible, a putrid stench I don't know how to describe. I asked Krista what it meant.

"He's probably septicemic," she said. "And hypoalbuminic. The kidneys and the liver shut down without water. He can't flush his toxins so they come out the skin, basically."

She gestured for the other technician to help her lift the dog out of the crate and onto the examination table. I took a step back, glad to know the dog was in good hands, but slightly anxious that there wasn't anything more I could do. I was slightly encouraged when Krista inserted an electronic thermometer into the dog's rectum and the dog lifted his head feebly, as if to say, "Hey—what's going on back there?" It was more motion than I'd seen in him so far.

The other technician had shaved a spot on the dog's left front leg, but she seemed to be having trouble finding a vein.

"What's his temperature?" I asked.

"Ninety-two," Krista said.

"What's normal?"

"About a hundred and two," she said, not looking up at me as she put drops in the dog's eyes. The second technician brought in an I.V. drip and then Krista inserted the needle, using surgical tape to hold it in place. They added medications to the drip. One bottle contained a drug called Baytril (enrofloxacin) and the other contained Ampicillin, which, I later learned, are both used to treat bacterial infections.

Then Dr. Roundtree entered the room. He was a man of medium height, maybe fifty years old, with dark hair, wearing a white shirt and blue tie beneath his white laboratory coat. He looked at the dog first, then at me, then back at the dog.

"Wow," he said. "What a pitiful sight."

My heart sank. I knew the vet had probably seen dogs in all kinds of conditions. He'd seen the worst, and the dog I'd brought in fit into that category before he'd even laid a hand on him.

"Where did you find him?" he asked me. I told him the name of the canyon. "When was this?"

"Yesterday afternoon," I said. "I got out of the canyon and got some water and dog food to bring him and went back in."

"What sort of dog food?"

I couldn't remember the brand, but I described the foul smelling glob of protein and fat I'd managed to set in front of the dog.

"He eat any?"

"Some," I said. "Was that the right thing to do?"

"Absolutely," he said. "It probably helped rehydrate him a little. Dry food wouldn't have done that."

He poked and prodded the dog, looking at his eyes, his teeth. He looked at the dog's foot pads and ran a finger across the dog's nose where a crust had formed.

"Looks like he might have had distemper at some point," Dr. Roundtree explained. "That's why his teeth look the way they do. Destroys the enamel."

He listened to the dog's heart with a stethoscope, and then he looked at his watch for ten seconds as he listened, writing down the dog's heart rate on a chart Krista had provided.

"What do you think?" I asked him, trying to sound hopeful.

"We'll have to wait and see," he said. "I'm worried about his white blood cell count. With malnutrition and dehydration this severe, we often see brain damage. It could be very minor or it could mean he's not going to pull through. There's actually a fairly broad spectrum of possibilities."

In a way, it felt worse now, because I still needed the dog to survive, but it was out of my hands. The dog's fate was in the right hands, but it left me feeling helpless.

Finally, Dr. Roundtree stepped away, and Krista and the other technician transferred the dog to another larger, padded crate before moving him to the recovery room.

"So how does the billing for this work?" I asked, dreading the answer.

Michelle and I had started a do-it-yourself garage called the Wrench-It Center, where we supplied the tools and equipment, based on an idea I had as a Marine where the military would let enlisted personnel work on their personal vehicles in the automotive shop, but the Wrench-It Center had turned from a do-it-yourself business into an awkward mix of self-service and full service, and it was foundering.

"We'll do what we can for the pup, but we'd like it if someone could assume financial responsibility," Dr. Roundtree said.

This was what I was afraid he would say. The idea that we could run up a huge tab, and then the dog wouldn't make it, was more than a little disheartening. I'd gone into the automotive repair business with my eyes wide open, knowing it was a gamble, but knowing what the odds and the stakes were, too. With the dog, I didn't know either.

"I'll take responsibility," I said.

"Fair enough," the vet said. "He's stabilized now. Do we have your contact information?"

"I don't know," I said.

"You can leave it with Krista so we can call you if anything changes."

He left. I found Krista at the reception desk and gave her both my home phone number and the number for my cell. When she asked me where I was staying in town, I said I didn't know. I thought it might be a good night to sleep beneath the stars.

"So what do you think?" I asked her. "I know it's probably hard to say, but what do you think his chances are?"

"You're right," she told me. "It's hard to say. When we see severe dehydration, sometimes the internal organs shut down, and even if we can restart them, they might be damaged. There could be brain damage. Seizures or convulsions. Maybe blindness. We'll keep an eye on him. The best I can say is fifty-fifty. He might make it, or he might have to be euthanized."

The word hit me like a punch in the stomach.

It was another emotional blow I hadn't anticipated. The feeling was physical, the way you might feel if you were in an elevator that suddenly drops two feet. I was now responsible for a life. This may be the way a new parent feels on the way home from the hospital with a new baby in a baby carrier in the back seat, overwhelmed and unprepared, with no turning back. That was ironic, considering the day before was Father's Day. New fathers, however, have nine months to get used to the idea, while I was being hit with it all at once. If the universe ran according to some kind of plan, then I had suddenly become part of that plan, and if there wasn't a plan, and every event was the result of a random roll of the dice, then I had reached in and changed the way the dice had landed. Everything was shifting. Nothing was simple any more.

I took a right out of the parking lot onto North Seventh Avenue to where it dead ended at Bureau Street, turned left, then took a right on Lake Powell Boulevard, past the Courtyard Marriott, until I hit 89 and open country. I asked myself as I drove, what was I going to do if the dog died?

Part of me thought, *No big deal. Dogs die all the time. It's not my dog, I did my part, and now it's out of my hands*. But that part was a lesser part of me, a voice I recognized, the one I used when I was trying to convince myself everything was going to be okay. The

Our Siberian husky Reagan. Could not have asked for a better best friend!

Sixth grade school photo. Times had been tough for me, but the next two years would be absolute hell.

Freshman year on the volleyball team. Won Most Improved. I was so proud of that award.

With my best friend's mom before prom my senior year. She filled an important gap in my life, for which I am forever grateful.

My fireteam in the Middle East, summer of 1997.

First time rappelling upside down in Singapore.

SPIE rigging over the Indian Ocean from underneath a helicopter.

Spring of 1998, Michelle and I finally met. This is overlooking Lake Elsinore.

Michelle and me, one week after I was discharged from the Marines.

Once again mesmerized in a beautiful slot.

Some technical work in my favorite canyon near Page.

First image I took of Riley in the pothole eating the food I picked up earlier in the day. This was the last time I saw him stand for a week.

A still image from the video I shot showing my ATV rigged up to anchor my rappel. The cat carrier is on the back.

A tense moment Monday morning. He was on the blanket I had left for him, but I didn't know if he was still alive.

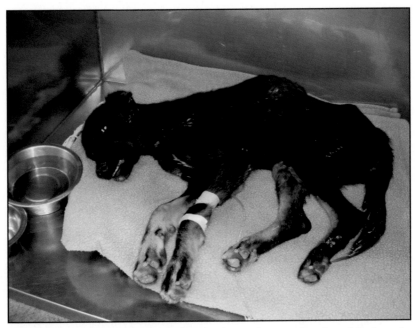

Tuesday morning in the Page Animal Hospital. I got him out, but these folks brought him back!

Friday, Riley was recovering at my friend's house in Park City. He lacked the muscle tone to hold his limbs in place.

Sunday morning at Jordenelle Reservoir, exactly one week after I found him.

July 10 with his new big brother, Kohi. Riley was officially part of the family and looking great!

The three of us had just arrived at Ellen's studio. What an experience!

Riley and Kohi on one of our many visits to the Colorado Plateau.

Now in Florida, Riley's taking things in stride, trying to "do as the locals do."

greater part of me knew I would be devastated, because it would mean evil had won after I'd vowed not to let it.

But something even bigger was going on.

I pulled over to the side of the road and got out of my truck when I realized I felt like I was about to cry. I was simultaneously struck with two questions, related but separate. I didn't understand exactly why I wanted to cry, and I didn't understand why I couldn't. The fact that a stray dog was deathly ill and might not make it through the night was a sad thought, but what was it to me? There were far worse things going on in the world that I could have been upset about. I didn't cry when my father died, so why now? Why this? I told myself I was just exhausted, and that I'd been holding my emotions in all day, and now they simply wanted to come out. I was labile or lachrymose, but it was just a result of fatigue.

Why I couldn't cry was slightly easier to understand. I didn't cry because I didn't know how to. That might sound odd, because it's something even newborn babies know to do, but I'd forgotten how . . . or maybe I'd trained myself not to. Growing up, I'd never seen anybody else do it. My mother seldom cried around me. I never saw my father, or my stepmother, shed a tear when I was a child. When I was little, having a wart removed at the doctor's office, the liquid nitrogen he used to freeze the wart stung like a thousand bees, but I didn't cry, and afterward, my mother told a coworker that she was surprised. I guess that was a sort of compliment. Boys generally get complimented for being "big" and "brave," even though crying is a natural emotional release, and no more so for girls than for boys. But for boys, it's not allowed. I'd never seen any value in crying, any up-side to it, when all it was likely to do was result in a scolding, or worse. Sure, when I was getting held down and beaten and bloodied up—or terrorized and chased through the streets—I may have shed a few tears, but in those moments, I had absolutely no control of the way my body was reacting to the circumstances surrounding it. Those tears were in response to the sheer terror I was feeling; they were not part of a conscious, emotional moment. Crying from sadness or grief is very different from crying hysterically because you're terrified.

"I have rules," I thought, there on the side of the road. "'No crying' is one."

I couldn't cry now because I'd told myself, my entire life, not to. And I couldn't cry because I worried that if I consciously made the decision to start now, I couldn't be sure I could ever stop. A dam would burst, and I needed to keep that dam in place. Otherwise, I might explode, and then melt into a puddle.

I didn't call Michelle right away because I knew she'd be at work. After dinner, I got back in my truck and went to a place I knew off Route 89, a viewpoint behind the Denny's restaurant with a spectacular view of the canyon, the dam, and Lake Powell to the north. There was a seven-hundred-foot drop to the river below with an easily crossed guardrail. The opposite side of the canyon was maybe three hundred yards away. The river below looked black from where I stood, no rapids that I could see, but I saw eddies and turbulence where the current had built up shoals of rock. Despite the incredible drop, you could actually hear the water flowing down below. The water was low, with only as much water flowing as the Glen Canyon Dam allowed.

I needed to think, absorb the landscape, and locate myself in it. I saw the cars crossing the bridge turn on their headlights, and the first few stars of early evening appeared in the blue overhead, while the sky in the west blazed with fire, the color that gave the cliffs their name. I witnessed the sky turn dark as the stars came out, the Milky Way a river of light above me. Traffic on 89 across the Glen Canyon Bridge slowed to a trickle. The dam was lit up like some kind of monument.

I took out my phone and called Michelle. I recounted the day's events, and what the vet had said.

"How are you doing?" she asked.

"Well," I began, "I've been better . . ." But I couldn't articulate what was going on. "The bottom line is, the dog is in the hospital. So I guess it's up to them. Or up to him."

"Did they say what they think his chances are?"

"Fifty-fifty," I said. "It depends. He may have to be euthanized."

I didn't have to say any more, and Michelle knew me well enough not to press. She knew me well enough to know what those words did to me. She understood me like no one else, which was why our marriage had endured owning and running two businesses together. She understood, as best she could, the trauma that had shaped me, and she knew why I would be so affected if we lost the puppy. The love we shared was strong, and as tangible over the phone as it would have been if she was there beside me.

"I'll talk to you later," I said, and then I hung up.

I kept the phone in my hand, thinking there was a chance that Michelle was going to call me back, worried about me. I knew, however, that she knew to leave me alone when I gave the signal that I needed to put some time and distance between me and what I was feeling. In a different place, I would go to the gym and lift weights until all I could think of was how tired I was.

She also knew me well enough to know how the dog in the canyon and I had something in common. We'd both been the victims of senseless cruelty. Maybe that explained why the dog's survival was so important to me—if he could survive, I could, too. But if he couldn't . . . In the desert, under a canopy of summer stars, I thought of the dog, for the first time, as another motherless creature. If he died, I knew I would take it personally. I would feel like I let him down, the way people let me down.

Then I'm ten, and my mother and I are at the mall, shortly before Christmas, and I have twenty dollars in my pocket, so I buy the game Battleship at Walgreens, but when I meet my mom in one of the restaurants at the mall, she says, "Nice going—Gary already got you that game." She could have told our neighbor, Gary, to return his present, rather than tell me to return mine. I feel deflated but know better than to ask her to help me return it, so I go back to Walgreens on my own. When the girl at Walgreens says she can only give me store credit, I get flustered and buy twenty dollars' worth of pure crap, candy and worthless plastic junk that I buy because I have to buy something and I'm running out of time.

When I return to the restaurant, my mother asks me what I bought. I show her. She tries hiding her laughter at my predicament, covering her mouth with her hand and snickering at me.

I'm ten, and my mother is laughing at me. . . .

5

I lay on an air mattress in the back of my truck, looking up at the night sky.

Most people think the brightest star in the sky is Polaris, or the North Star. It's not. It's Sirius, or the Dog Star, for its place in the constellation Canis Major, the Greater Dog. It's the brightest because it's also (after the sun) the closest, and getting closer. To my mind, it's a stretch of the imagination to see a dog in Canis Major, which is basically a Y with a leg at one of the ends of the Y and another leg at the solo end. Both legs are about the same length and pointing in the same direction, but it could be any animal with four legs and a long neck. People see what they want to see.

That night, waiting to find out if the dog was going to make it, I was finally able to see the four-legged animal in the constellation. I thought of all the other ways the word "dog" was used in the English language, and it struck me that most of them applied to or resonated with me. "Die like a dog," as in what I wanted the kids who tormented me to do. "Sick as a dog," as in how I felt so many times as a kid when I was afraid to go to school. "Dog eat dog," as in how the world seemed to me, and I was definitely the underdog in that regard. "Every dog has its day," as in what I was still waiting for. "Dog tired," as in what I felt physically. "Let sleeping dogs lie," as in what some people thought I should do. If that phrase meant letting go of the things that hurt me, I couldn't live up to it, because I wasn't holding onto them; they were holding on to me. One last one: "It's not the size of the dog in the fight—it's the size of the fight in the dog," an adage I'd learned to apply, and adopt, almost as a slogan, but at great cost.

My favorite word, though, was "dogged," meaning tenacious, stalwart, and untiring. I'd read about researchers who put heart monitors on sled dogs to see what sort of heart rates they were able to sustain over long distances. The researchers were shocked to learn dogs could sustain heart rates of three hundred beats per minute for hours, which was astonishing because scientists had previously thought the only mammals capable of sustaining three hundred beats per minute were tiny ones like mice or shrews. It explains how a pack of wolves can run down an elk, even though elk are faster than wolves. Wolves can outlast anything. I told myself the dog in the hospital had heart, in both senses of the word. I hoped it was enough.

Then I told myself I did, too. Surviving my childhood wouldn't have been possible without it.

I grew up in Cudahy, Wisconsin, which is on the western shore of Lake Michigan, on Milwaukee's "sout' side." You don't pronounce the "th." It's about five square miles, with a population of about twenty-four thousand people, mostly white. The beaches are rocky and the water is freezing cold, with weather-beaten concrete breakers every couple hundred yards that constantly fight a losing battle against the waves and the winter ice off the lake, and woods laced with bike paths on the bluffs above the beaches.

General Mitchell International Airport abuts the town to the west, putting the town, every few minutes, directly in the flight paths of low-flying airplanes taking off or landing, depending on the wind direction, but when you live there, you get so used to it you hardly notice.

The town was founded by a guy named Patrick Cudahy, who built a meatpacking plant/slaughterhouse that suffered a large fire in 2009, on the Fourth of July, as irony would have it. The fire put about a tenth of the town out of work. Apparently a couple of local kids were shooting off illegal fireworks and one landed on the building and burned a hole through the roof, which sounds exactly like something that would happen in Cudahy. There's a massive foundry for Ladish Forging that runs half the length of town, on Packard Avenue, that makes castings and machined titanium parts for the aerospace industry. The other big employer is Bucyrus-Erie in South Milwaukee, the neighboring town to the south, where they make the giant strip-mining shovels, the ones that chop the tops off mountains. It seems like there's a bar on virtually every corner, places called Rollie's Tap or Vnuk's Lounge or Sparky's, filled with Polish guys with hardworking hands and maybe axle grease under their fingernails and burn holes in their Carhartt overalls. My first "real" job was working for such a man, a concrete mason named Bob who was truly a hardass. Not having a father in my life, I found his temper and directness pretty intimidating.

People didn't drive fancy luxury cars in Cudahy, at least not when I grew up. They drove station wagons, minivans, and cars that were quickly and badly rusted from the winter road salt. I was thirteen when I saw my first BMW, and I assumed the driver must be rich. If you ride a motorcycle in Cudahy, and you probably do, it had better be a Harley, because they're made in Milwaukee. The people who live there think of themselves, accurately, as hardworking and straightforward, connoisseurs of life's simple pleasures, with traditional family values. To be fair, I can't criticize an entire town just because I have some horrible memories there. I also have some truly incredible memories, like falling in love for the first time, exploring the steep lakeside cliffs as a kid, or qualifying for the state swim meet my senior year. But the difficult years at home and at school tend to discolor the rosy memories I do have. The most traumatic and difficult times of my life happened in Cudahy. Sometimes it's hard to think fondly of my time there.

My house was an ugly five-unit apartment building on East Barnard, set close to the sidewalk. The front of the building was brown brick and featured lots of windows. The paint peeled from the window trim. There was a weird gap between the two front apartments, as if they'd originally built two houses close together, then added the rear apartments. The neighborhood was squarely middle-class, though it looks worse today than it did then. We were not wealthy, and it showed. I had my own room, with a mattress on the floor instead of a bed, and a poster of a white Lamborghini on the wall. I was probably the only kid in town who had his own filing cabinet. I didn't keep files in it, but rather special books, souvenirs, and various artifacts. My musical tastes were eclectic and changed over time. In seventh grade, I went through a phase where I listened to Mozart on my boom box, but later my tastes transitioned to music a bit more lively, Metallica and Slayer. I had a fascination with some rather colorful reading material, which I kept in my filing cabinet, titles like *Poor Man's James Bond*, written by a man named Kurt Saxon who is credited with coining the term "survivalist," and *The Anarchist's Cookbook*, written by a man named William Powell who has, since its publication, become a devout Christian who's tried to have the book removed from publication. I can't say precisely what drew me to these types of books. In spite of everything I went through, I did not have revenge fantasies. I found in them a way to escape reality, but also, ways to fantasize about having and exercising power. I believed that one day I would be in the military, shooting firearms and possibly working with explosives. Those books reassured me that such a future was possible.

My father, Mark Anderegg, was competent and respected at work, but at home, he could be cold, arrogant, narcissistic, crude, and downright mean—in short, a bully. As he aged, his hair changed from dark to salt and pepper, and he had a close-cropped beard his entire adult life. He was probably just shy of morbidly obese, with a massive beer belly, and he wore wire-rimmed gradient eyeglasses that turned dark in the sunlight but never seemed to turn entirely clear indoors. He also, frequently, wore bandanas as head bands, though his hair was never long enough that he needed to hold it back from his face, and he seldom did anything strenuous enough to work up a sweat. While married to my mother, albeit briefly, he told his coworkers she'd tricked him into getting her pregnant. "I hate kids," he would later tell Michelle. "I didn't want to have anything to do with Zak until he was sixteen." He was cheating on my mother, Sandra, with Robin before they divorced, and he later cheated on Robin, or so I was told. Any semblance of cordiality between my mother and father ended when she was forced to sue him for falling behind on his child support payments.

Robin was also overweight, with large thighs and fleshy upper arms. She had a pale pinkish complexion, an up-turned nose, eyes that narrowed as though she were frequently squinting, and a small mouth set in a face that was broad and round.

Robin resented me because I was the baggage that came attached to Mark. After my mother sued Mark for child support, the contempt he and Robin had towards Sandra increased, a hatred that Robin took out on me.

Sandra was my primary caregiver, though she was, by any measure, a mess. She was also overweight, with a weak chin and a prominent overbite, blue eyes that drooped and made her look sleepy, eyebrows that were so light as to be barely noticeable above her narrow wire-rimmed glasses, thin light brown hair that hung straight down to her jawline like a helmet, and bangs. She came from Polish and German extraction, raised in a strict Catholic household and educated at a Catholic school by nuns who were, as she described them, harsh on a good day and sadistic on a bad one.

A child, of course, sees his parents through a child's eyes and interprets parental behaviors in a child's terms; yet even then, it seemed to me, though I couldn't explain it or understand it, that she did not know how to love. It was just like the way some people can't carry a tune or tell a joke or cook a meal. She wasn't like other moms I knew, and our relationship was not like the relationships other boys had with their moms. We were more like squabbling siblings than parent and child. If there was supposed to be some sort of parental authority she had over me, she never established it, or she was too timid to assert it. I did not try to please her or win her love because she couldn't express love in a way that made me want it.

Instead of hugging me or holding my hand as I crossed the street, she would sit on me and pin me to the floor by the wrists and say, "Tell me you love me." If I said it, it was only to get her off me. In truth, I felt scared and trapped when I was around her.

Her inability to understand what I was experiencing at school, as the victim of a prolonged bullying campaign, was entirely consistent with the way she dealt with the feelings of others. She was cognizant of the way they felt, but she was incapable of honoring these feelings when it conflicted with her condition, her OCD. She was, for example, utterly incapable of ever being on time, for anything, anywhere, ever, despite any and all efforts she made to be punctual. She worked for a doctor for almost thirteen years and she was late for work over half the time, until, when I was in seventh grade, the doctor finally had to warn her that if she was late again, he'd have no choice but to fire her. Most people would find a way to be on time, but my mother could not. After she was fired, she spent nine months on the couch, depressed. She lost job after job for the same reason, sabotaging herself over and over again, but each time she would say only, "I don't know what my deal is—I meant to be on time—I failed again," incurring punishment and punishing herself without apparently realizing that being chronically late wasn't just about her—it was, quite simply, rude to the people who expected her to be on time. This wasn't enough to get her to change her behavior, though.

And so we fought, day in, day out, about what I should wear, what I needed to do, how I combed my hair or didn't comb my hair. They were never, to be clear, substantive disputes over whether a movie was appropriate for children my age, or if I needed a second helping of whatever was for dinner. Instead, there were violent efforts, at least on my part, to have my feelings recognized and validated—to be heard, and seen.

Once, when we fought in public, she decided she would teach me a lesson. I was in fourth grade. I don't remember what we were fighting about, but when we got to the car, she unlocked her door and got in but didn't unlock mine, and then she drove off without me. She came back for me, but I'd felt completely abandoned and alone. She did this on multiple occasions, until eventually I'd had enough. The next time she tried it, I ripped the radio antenna off as she pulled away, which embarrassed her because a man in a nearby car had witnessed the scene.

I knew only to be afraid of her anger and her irrational behaviors. That fear translated quickly into hatred, because she was supposed to be someone I could count on, and she was not. At first, I hated how lonely I felt, how unseen and unheard and isolated I was, but that sort of loneliness can turn into a kind of armor you wear and embrace. You realize that if you're on your own, so be it. You decide you can't depend on anyone, so you depend on yourself.

Because Sandra worked nine to five, I had a series of babysitters up until I was in about sixth grade. At that point, I was old enough to let myself in and take care of myself in the empty house. Calling it an empty house makes it sound like something I dreaded, but the opposite was true. I liked it. I could do anything I wanted to. Too often, to my regret, what I wanted to do was plunk myself down in front of the television in the rocking chair with a Coke and a bag of potato chips and watch reruns of '80s sitcoms like *Family Ties* or *Gimme a Break* or *Duck Tales,* which was about Donald Duck's nephews, Huey, Dewey and Louie, though Scrooge McDuck was in it more than Donald was. If I had a time machine and could go back and redo those after-school hours, there are surely ways I could put them to better use.

Feeling lonely wasn't all bad, because lonely meant safe. It's hard to remember exactly when or how it started. I wasn't antisocial, at least not at first. I was in the Cub Scouts, and the Boy Scouts. I played on sports teams. I played with my cousins at family gatherings. But it was a label I wore, at school, and it was the same label, year after year. I felt like I carried the label with me, the stigma, wherever I went. How is someone's social standing established in kindergarten? I dressed like everyone else. I acted like everyone else. . . .

It started out as verbal chastising, and it seemed to get worse, or more entrenched, with every passing grade. I was able to tell myself that life is just like that, some kids are more popular than others, and if somebody had to be the most popular, then somebody had to be the least popular, and that was me, but I couldn't make sense of it. No kid should ever have to experience that.

Each time it happened, the wound reopened, and it was like hitting your shin over and over again in the exact same spot. The wound never healed, and the pain got worse. To endure it, I'd lock myself into a kind of mental or emotional survival mode, but the simple act of bracing myself was traumatizing. Trauma is what happens to you, to your mind and perhaps to your soul, when you can neither fight nor flee. Those are the two options Nature gives animals in the wild. A kid on a school bus can't flee, and he can't fight. When someone called me a name, I'd laugh and pretend I thought it was funny, too. I'd retreat into myself, but not too far because if you retreat too far, you get attacked again. It's like the advice you get about what to do when you encounter a bear on a hiking trail or a mean dog on the street—don't run, because if you do, you just invite them to chase you—just curl up in a ball and play dead. On the school bus, I couldn't hide, and I had to keep an eye on the people teasing me, but the fifteen-minute trip was torture. Nice way to start the day.

Early grade school was tolerable, if not particularly fun, the abuse mainly verbal. Kids called me names, and after school, I was never welcomed to hang out with them or invited on play dates. I lost sleep, trying to figure out why it was happening. The stress actually made me sick. I had insomnia. I developed a hyper-vigilance because I felt like I was on display all the time, conspicuous and singled out.

In grade school, there'd been a kid named Scott and another kid named Joey. In seventh grade, there was Ben and a different guy also named Scott, and then Leona and Jerry. I always wondered what they said about me when I wasn't present, because the bullying seemed so coordinated or organized, as though there was a group consensus. Any day, any one of them could drop a comment. It felt like a wolf pack, where one harasses the prey while the others rest and prepare for when it's their turn.

It's an insidious sense of constant betrayal, where you don't know who your real friends are, or when your enemies are going to do something. I once ran into Scott in the boys' room at school in fifth grade, and to my surprise, we chatted pleasantly, as though nothing had ever happened between us. I had the sense he thought, "You're not cool, but I'll talk to you as long as we're alone—in front of people, I'm going to have to pick on you again, to show everybody we're not friends." He was athletic and he had a reputation for being tough, so a lot of people followed him with the sense that it was probably smarter to be his friend than his enemy. Joey was an Italian kid who was sort of charismatic and made everybody laugh, all piss and vinegar, and he was Scott's friend. Running into either of them, separately, wasn't nearly as dangerous as meeting them together, when they aided and abetted each other, as though competing to see who could be meaner to me. Meeting them alone, I almost had the feeling they were embarrassed by the way they behaved toward me, as close as I would get to an admission that they knew what they were doing was wrong.

In ninth grade, when I was a Boy Scout, I was nominated for the Order of the Arrow. It's a nice thing to earn, because the boys who get it have been chosen by their scout leaders and recognized as representing the ideals scouting supposedly stands for: honesty and hard work and fellowship and service. When I learned of the possibility of receiving the award, I said I didn't want it, because to receive it, you have to participate in a ceremony where you have to stand up in front of the entire summer camp of around 250 boys, and that idea terrified me. What if someone said something, called me a name, or made a fart noise while I stood alone in front of everybody?

Lying in the back of my pickup truck outside of Page, Arizona, I thought about the dog in the hospital. The word "dogged" means never giving up. There had to be something more than a cardio-vascular system capable of sustaining three hundred beats per minute to explain doggedness, some sort of innate stubbornness, or maybe indefatigable optimism, that kept them running. Nature had to select for the gene that let them believe, against all odds, that the chase was going to pay off, a persistence of hope.

I'm in tenth grade, and everything shifts in a single instance when I see a thirty-second commercial for the Navy SEALs. It's much like a light turns on or a door opens in my mind. It's another way out of my misery that won't be easy, but won't require killing myself. It's a way to reinvent myself and channel my energies and abilities, and more than anything else, a way to get the hell out of Cudahy as soon as I'm old enough to enlist. It's hope. I want to be a Navy SEAL, and I know that if I'm going to be a Navy SEAL, I'm going to have to change my body by lifting weights.

I am actually pretty decent at sports and I am on the volleyball and tennis teams, so I am already reasonably fit, but I know there's a very high drop-out rate for guys training to be SEALs. Having a clear goal—this goal—to work toward appeals to my logical engineering brain. I'm an okay swimmer, but if I'm to become a SEAL, I need to join the swim team to really take things to the next level. I join my sophomore year. It's the hardest thing, physically, and in some ways emotionally, that I've ever done. I'm the worst swimmer on the team, at first, enduring agonizingly long practices and on several occasions nearly drowning as I learn how to swim freestyle competitively. I am nearly "one of the guys" on the team, but after practice ends for the night, or between seasons, they largely ignore me because of the stigma attached to who I am.

There's a gap between the swim season and the tennis season, so I have the time after school to use the school's weight room. The problem is that the weight room is where all the "cool" jocks hang out, and thus it's a minefield for someone in my position at the bottom of the social totem pole, an endeavor fraught with peril. Fortunately, I know a guy named Pete who, while not as unpopular as me, is by no means part of the "in" crowd. I've known him since kindergarten, and nobody messes with him because he holds a black belt in tae kwon do. I'm in the weight room one day, avoiding the free weights section where all the hardcore lifters congregate, working with one of the pull-down machines. I set the weight low and begin operating the machine, all my emotional shields raised, expecting to catch some sort of trouble. While trying to look straight ahead and not make eye contact with anybody, I hear a voice say, "You're doing that all wrong."

I brace myself, but fortunately, it's Pete. He asks me if I need a workout partner, and it's fairly obvious that I do. He asks me if I want him to make me a workout schedule with a plan—day one, day two. This is exactly what I need. The progress I make is almost immediate, maybe because I'm starting from zero. By the second week, I'm lifting more than I did the first. After a month, I'm lifting more than many of the guys in the weight room and, specifically, more than some of the jerks who've teased me. When I tell my tennis coach I'm going to quit the tennis team to spend more time lifting weights, he can't believe it. He says I have the potential to be one of the best players on the team by my senior year. I don't care, because my goal is to be a Navy SEAL, not a tennis player. I can see and feel my body responding to the regimen. Eventually I'm benching more than two hundred pounds, which is considerably more than the "cool" kids are lifting.

I start feeling competitive, knowing I'm stronger than them. The bench press is more or less the "showcase" in any locker room. I'll see one of the "cool" guys lifting, and when he's done, I'll move to the bench he was on and add weight to whatever he was lifting, before rolling the bar off the rack and lifting it. There is no argument they can make—the "loser" is lifting more than they were, so apparently the loser isn't a loser any more. There is, I'm learning firsthand, some sort of deeply embedded code of masculinity where the perception of strength commands respect, like some species of bird where the male with the longest beak or the largest bib markings holds dominance over other males with shorter beaks or smaller bibs. I realize I don't have to fight anybody—I just have to look like I could fight anybody.

My attitude changes along with my body. I'm learning things about myself. It's more than just what others are seeing in me. I am surprising myself, seeing what my body can do, and what my spirit is capable of. I'm concentrating like I've never concentrated before, developing a kind of personal intensity. I am actually feeling confident for the first time in my life. As a consequence, the bullying stops almost immediately. Somehow, I've been able to convert inner strength and pain into outer strength and gain. It's not that the bullies have developed a new respect for me—it's that I've developed a new respect for myself.

It happens bit by bit, slowly, day by day.

After I started training for the Navy SEALs, I started bicycling long distances, as much as thirty miles a day, both to get in shape and to get out of the house and away from the dysfunction there. On my bicycle, I wasn't just improving my aerobic conditioning— I was also alone and safe, and I could relax in the way your brain shifts into neutral when your body is working hard. It meant a lot to me, not just because it told me I'd done well, but because it told everybody else I had.

Later, after receiving the news that my less-than-perfect eyesight would keep me from attaining my goal of being a Navy SEAL, I became a Marine. In boot camp, I was briefly promoted to "Guide," not an actual rank but a position of leadership among equals. However, a few days later I was demoted when, on a forced march, a soldier from the platoon ahead of us lagged behind, and my drill instructor ordered me to push the poor kid out of the way and I refused. We'd been taught, after all, that our mission was to save and protect our fellow Marines. When I was offered the position of Guide again a few days later, I turned him down, much to his amazement, but I'd lost all respect for him, which made the recognition and promotion meaningless.

In a way, working out in the gym with weights merged perfectly with joining the Marines, which presented me with a life that was absolutely regimented and predictable and perfect for maintaining a training routine. I was soon in such good physical condition that I acquired the nickname "Android" (from my last name) from my peers, a name I embraced and identified with. The week I left the Marines, I tested myself. I completed a three-mile run in a time of 17:29. I could bench press 350 pounds. I could press a pair of 100-pound dumbbells over my head five times, and I could bench press a pair of 120-pound dumbbells ten times, all at a bodyweight of 211 pounds. The satisfaction I got was not a matter of vanity or the desire to acquire bragging rights, though when you're living with a bunch of gung-ho Marines, it's rather natural to compete with each other in all kinds of ways, including weightlifting. What mattered more to me, much more, was measuring how far I'd come from the first time I'd set foot in the weight room at school when Pete had offered to help me. Or rather, how far I'd come from well before I ever set foot in a gym, when I saw myself as the proverbial ninety-five-pound weakling getting sand kicked in his face at the beach.

It was in Marine Corps boot camp that I first learned to rappel, which began inauspiciously when I stood at the top of a sixty-foot wall while the instructor screamed at me (again with the screaming) to go over the side. So I did, but I forgot to lock my knees and slammed hard into the wall. I had remembered, however, not to release my braking hand and avoided a free fall and certain death. You don't get points in the Marines for trying. The instructor yelled, "See what happens when you don't lock your legs?"

I haven't made that mistake since then, which tells me that sometimes screaming helps.

We later trained off a seventy-five-foot tower at a base in Singapore. When the instructor, a Lieutenant Farnum, saw my enthusiasm, he asked me if I wanted to learn to rappel upside down. I wasn't sure if it would ever come in handy, but it sounded like fun. The feat is accomplished by lowering yourself ten feet or so from the top and then rotating your body clockwise until your feet are above your head and your right arm is pointing straight towards the ground. To this day, I enjoy rappelling upside down because it is simply exhilarating. Looking straight down, maybe a hundred feet or more, and controlling your fear is something that energizes me.

If I learned nothing else as a Marine, I learned how to conquer my fears. When we learned during the same deployment that some CH-46 helicopter pilots needed to practice inserting and extracting combat troops using a long line with D-rings attached to it, I volunteered, and half an hour later, I was hanging from a rope from the bottom of a helicopter that was flying several hundred feet above the Indian Ocean at a forward airspeed of maybe sixty-five knots. Given the circumstances, it seemed like a perfect opportunity to practice my air-guitar.

Being a Marine means learning to suppress your feelings. In one sense, it might seem I'd have been a natural at it. Part of making a man, or perhaps more accurately a boy, into an effective soldier requires that he learns to conquer a number of things in himself, including his fears and his self-imposed limitations. For example, part of my training led me to CWSS training, which stands for Combat Water Safety Swimmer. It's designed to teach you how to save your fellow Marines during shore landings where you have to negotiate large waves and rip tides, all while wearing heavy gear. When I was on the swim team in high school, I was competitive at the state level and could turn in winning times at distances anywhere between fifty and five hundred yards. Rescue swimming, however, was an entirely different endeavor, because it meant taking tough Marines, guys who generally think they're badasses with something to prove, and pushing them past their breaking points.

On the last day of training, we had to execute mock rescues, with the instructors posing as victims. When it was my turn, I jumped in after my "victim," but immediately found it challenging to swim with just my legs, using my arms to secure the "victim." Then, just as I dove down and locked my arms around him, he used his hands to push against the water and drive us down, something you'd think a genuine drowning victim wouldn't do. When I finally managed to surface with him, I let out an explosive breath and gasped to take as much new air in as possible, and then we were below the surface again. We surfaced three times, until I thought I was going hypoxic. When I finally managed to swim with him toward the edge of the pool, I lost control of him and he started to sink, while three instructors on the edge of the pool screamed at me, telling me my victim was going to either drown or suffer from brain damage. The idea was to reproduce the stress of an actual combat situation, and it played all kinds of tricks on my brain.

I managed to pass the test, but also nearly passed out. You know it's valuable, because if the time comes and you're the one who ends up being the victim, you want to know the men around you won't panic, but it exacts a heavy cost on your mental well-being because suppressing all those feeling only means they come back to bite you twice as hard at some later opportunity. I could say, honestly, that for better or worse, the Marines provided me with an environment to mature into a man in a way nothing else I know of could do, and I am extremely grateful for the experience.

Lying in the back of my truck, gazing up at the sky above the Colorado Plateau, I realized it's both the size of the dog in the fight *and* the size of the fight in the dog, but the size of the fight in the dog comes first. That spark, that persistence gene, that little tenaciously optimistic bit, is what drives the dog to get stronger, to keep running and build muscles as it runs. The spark had almost died inside me, but at the last minute, almost in the nick of time, I found a way to tap into it. There was an ember inside me, buried deep beneath the accumulated ashes, and I was able to bring it back to life and then feed the fire until it blazed.

I hoped the puppy I found could do it, too. If he survived, he was, by nature and by definition, more dogged than I would ever be.

6

The next morning at the Page Animal Hospital, Dr. Roundtree was busy, and a girl I didn't recognize was sitting behind the desk, but Krista was there. She smiled when she saw me.

"How's he doing?" I asked.

"Better than he was yesterday," she said, "but we're not out of the woods. You wanna see?"

She led me down the hall to a room full of cages. I knew which cage was his because only one had an IV drip stand outside of it. I'd expected some kind of isolated ICU, the way emergency patients might be treated in a hospital. I felt like I should have donned latex gloves or a hospital gown first. Krista told me he'd gone through an entire drip bag overnight and was on his second. He had wet himself, too, which was promising, but there were still other concerns, such as possible permanent cognitive impairment and organ damage, most likely the kidneys.

"He also had a weak bowel movement this morning, the consistency of tar," she told me.

I understood that renal failure was usually fatal. I had a dog at home, an Australian blue heeler named Kohi, and I knew a bit about dog health in general. I knew that grapes and raisins were poisonous to dogs, for example. Scientists aren't exactly sure why this is; they simply know that grapes or raisins can cause renal tubule necrosis, destroying the small conduits the kidneys use to filter and break down toxins and produce urine. When the kidney can't make urine to flush the toxins, there's no hope, unless, I supposed, you could put a dog on a kidney machine, which I was sure people with a lot of money did, but I wasn't people with a lot of money.

"Go ahead and open the door if you want," she told me.

I knelt down in front of the cage and opened the door. He still smelled, and he looked horrible, lying on his side, covered in mud with the catheter taped to his paw. I supposed, on a healthier dog, they might have put one of those big plastic cones around his neck to keep him from chewing on the catheter, but with this dog, no such precaution was necessary. This dog lacked the strength to move as he stared off into space, seemingly immobile. However, when I knelt down, he wagged his tail. Just the tip of it—just once, rising an inch off the mat before falling back.

To me, the tiny tail wag was a brave thumbs up, the kind you see when they carry a previously unconscious football player off the field on a stretcher. Before he goes into the locker room, he gives the crowd a sign to tell them he's going to be alright, and the crowd cheers. The crowd inside me cheered, too. I wanted to believe not only that he was giving me a positive signal, but also that he recognized me somehow. It might have been simply an acknowledgment that someone, anyone, was there next to him, maybe even an involuntary reflex. As far as I could tell, the dog had been virtually unconscious the day before, but I knew that dogs have incredible noses and can identify smells thousands of times better than people can. By the time I'd worked up a sweat climbing out of the canyon, I must have been fairly identifiable.

"Has he moved at all?" I asked.

"Nope," a technician told me. "We've been moving him every couple of hours to keep him from getting sore. He's on his second bag of fluids though, so that's good."

I was wary of anthropomorphizing the animal. People think that when a dog licks your face, he's giving you a kiss, bestowing affection—what he's doing, according to the experts, is exhibiting a common pup behavior where juvenile canines lick the mother's lips to encourage her to regurgitate food for them to subsequently eat. We make inferences and project our own emotions onto dogs, coloring our interpretations of how they behave and why. I think it's important to try to understand a dog on a dog's terms. Yet, it struck me as remarkable how closely those terms parallel our own, where we—man and dog—have somehow learned to communicate with each other in a way no two species ever have. I don't know if we learned their language, more than they learned ours, but the point remains that both sides tried.

The first evidence anthropologists have to document the relationship between men and dogs dates back to about thirty thousand years ago, when early man lived in small tribal groups or villages that were, if not permanent habitations, occupied for several seasons, long enough to build up a residue of garbage, including discarded animal bones from which the early canines scavenged and fed. In North America, the wolf sat at the top of the food chain, at least until the early humans made it across the land bridge from Siberia, and then wolves and humans competed for the position. Then someone, somehow, one of us, or maybe both of us, signaled for a truce.

If you watch how one dog meets another unfamiliar dog, you can typically observe a pattern of behavior where, as the dogs come rushing in to meet, face-to-face, they both stiffen up. This is a tentative moment, one in which they try to assess, "Are you friendly or do I have to be on guard?" When the tails wag to signal a mutual acceptance of the rules of engagement the two dogs slowly circle in to sniff each other's butts. Some kind of signal must have transpired, thirty thousand years ago, between man and dog, giving each other permission to approach. It may have been a wag of a tail.

We had reasons to fear each other. We still fear each other, even though wolves have more reason to fear us than we have to fear them. It may have been that the first wolves to approach the human garbage dumps and campfires were puppies, juveniles who hadn't yet learned to be afraid. Ethnologists describe the differences between how wolves and dogs behave as paedomorphism, meaning a kind of incomplete or partial evolution where the adult of one species imitates the juvenile characteristics of another. Adult dogs will sit, stay, obey commands, wait to be fed, and bond with other species, as will juvenile wolves. Mature wolves won't do any of those things, which is why they can't be kept as pets. The juvenile wolves we adopted, thirty thousand years ago, may have retained their juvenile characteristics simply because they had no reason not to—as long as we kept them fed and happy, why fix what wasn't broken? While working at the Institute of Cytology and Genetics in Novosibirsk, Russia, a scientist named Dmitri Belyaev bred wild foxes by choosing the tamest among them (the ones that allowed humans to approach them) and was able to domesticate them in about forty generations, rendering the foxes that resulted as quite "dog-like." Humans and dogs have been living together for perhaps fifteen thousand generations, working, for thirty millennia, to understand and collaborate with each other.

I'm not an expert in these things. My hope is just to explain why I felt connected to the puppy. It could have been entirely my imagination, but if it was, I was imagining the same thing the first Cro-Magnon man imagined when the first juvenile wolf stepped from the darkness into the light of the campfire. My sense, leaning down to pet the dog in the crate with the IV drip in him, was that he understood something—not that he understood something about me, but that we both understood the same thing. He'd been abused and abandoned, left to die, and maybe he hadn't put it all together yet, but if someone could transport him to the bottom of a canyon and leave him there to die, it was reasonable for him to assume that I could also be a threat to him. But he wasn't threatened by me. He wagged his tail to tell me that, somehow, he knew I was trustworthy. That he was willing to give mankind another chance.

I wondered if the dog experienced stress, and the release from stress, the same way I did. Once on a previous wilderness excursion, when I'd gotten lost in the mountains near Los Angeles in the snow—without adequate food, water, or clothing—I went into a survival mode, my only focus on finding the road I'd somehow lost. From that focus, I derived a kind of calmness or composure, but once I was safe and back on the road, all the emotions I'd been suppressing caught up to me, and only then did I realize or appreciate how close I'd come to getting myself into serious trouble. Maybe the dog was having a similar delayed reaction, and only now, safe and in good hands, could he let his guard down.

I wondered, seeing him lying in the crate, what made a lone wolf separate from the pack. Did he not fit in, or did he choose to go out on his own? I assumed it was the former. Maybe they were wolves who for some reason failed to recognize the signals, didn't wag their tails soon enough or often enough, or didn't notice when more dominant wolves did? Then I wondered what would happen if two lone wolves met. Would they fight, or would they empathize with each other and realize they had something in common? Would they realize they'd be better off if they teamed up?

Would they wag their tails or bare their teeth?

"He's exhausted," Krista said, looking over my shoulder.

On my way out, I looked into a room off to the side and saw Dr. Roundtree, who was in the middle of some sort of surgical procedure on a cat. The cat, black with white paws and cowl, was lying on its back with a tube down its throat, and some of his internal organs had been lifted from his chest cavity to make room for the veterinarian to do whatever it was he was doing. It may sound odd to think a former US Marine sergeant might feel squeamish around blood and gore, but I had to suppress a brief gag reflex. I should have been tougher, in theory, but, in truth, I've always been queasy around blood. In third grade, I attached a fake bloody eyeball from a costume shop to my forehead for Halloween, but when I looked in the mirror, the sight of the eye and the fake blood actually caused me to see stars and almost faint. I was reminded that the animal hospital was a portal, a place where sick animals came; some or most went home better, but some didn't make it. It happened every day. It happened no matter how skilled the surgeon or how lucky the patient.

I left the animal hospital thinking about the cat and feeling like I was covered in a thick coating of gloom that I desperately wanted to rinse off. I needed to get my mind off it all. If I was back home in Salt Lake City, I probably would have gone to a gym to work it off, but of course, I was surrounded by opportunities for exercise. I made a quick stop at the first grocery store I saw to load up on water and snacks, and then I headed out of town for a slot canyon a little over five miles from Page I'd seen on a map, far enough to get away from people but close enough to get back quickly if I felt the need.

Thankfully, no two slot canyons are the same. I hoped I wasn't going to find another puppy in this one, because I wasn't sure I could handle it. At the truck, I pared down my gear and took only enough rope for a rappel or two. The first fifty yards or so was a flat wash, deep sand that had my calves and thighs burning in fifteen or twenty paces. As the canyon sloped down, the sand gave way to petrified sand dunes called "slick rock," because the iron shoes on the horses of the pioneers who discovered the region slipped against the surface, which is actually more like rough sandpaper. Mountain bikers, however, love riding on slick rock because of the grip they get with their fat, rubber tires. The bottoms of my hiking boots found similar purchase.

I walked sure-footed and easily along a winding half-pipe of stone that grew narrower the longer I traveled. My eye followed the striations in the water-worn rock as the walls rose vertically to either side of me, as though I were walking in the trough of a frozen ocean wave. The canyon curved and undulated, winding its way through the sediment in dips and twists, and after a while I felt like I were lost in some sort of interactive sculptural art form, flowing into it along the contours.

After perhaps two or three hundred yards, the declivity carved sharply down another fifty yards before terminating at a sixty-foot drop into a much larger canyon. In a rainstorm, I would have been standing at the top of a large waterfall, though if there was water raging down the canyon, I wouldn't stand there for long. Slot canyons are all, one way or another, tributary canyons feeding into Lake Powell or the Grand Canyon, so many arms and branches and forks that I'm not sure they all have names. From a hot air balloon or a helicopter, or using a program like Google Earth, you'd see a latticework of ravines and washes and veins all draining into the Colorado River and eventually the Gulf of California. From the air, you'd be able to see how all these cracks in the earth converge and lead to a single point, like a mathematical equation or a logical syllogism solvable with deductive reasoning. From the ground inside one of these tributaries, or more accurately from below the ground, you are a mouse in a maze, and all you can see are the impenetrable walls around you and a path that opens and closes to you.

I left the first canyon, Canyon A, to explore the rim of the second, Canyon B, looking for a place where I might drop in. After about fifteen easy minutes on slick rock, I arrived at a slope where Canyon B met Canyon C and edged down an incline until the angle was too steep to walk. There I drilled a hole, set a bolt, donned my harness, and set my rope. Once in Canyon C, I removed my harness and gear and left it there, thinking I was not in the mood for hardcore exploring, and that if I hit a drop-off, I'd just turn back. I headed downstream, ignoring any number of side canyons, and explored for about three hours, seeing things I'd seen on other trips elsewhere, logjams and holding pools and miniature stone arches, and things that shouldn't be there, like a weather worn deflated soccer ball, as well as things I'd never seen before, including one canyon absolutely clogged with a dense mat of tumbleweeds. You see tumbleweeds blowing across the landscape in cowboy movies and think of them as archetypal images of the American West without realizing many of them, maybe most of them, are not native to this continent and arrived from Asia or Russia as unwanted hitchhikers in seed shipments. The mechanism of seed distribution has always been, to my mind, one of nature's more ingenious adaptations, where, in a dry climate, the top part of a plant dies and breaks off, then rolls across the arid topography in the wind, distributing seeds and spores as it tumbles before eventually, like a steel ball in a pachinko game, coming to rest in a low spot where there is likely to be water. When the water cracks open the seed, the plant comes alive again. The botanical term for this classification of plants using this method of propagation is *diaspore*.

The hiker's term for finding a canyon clogged with tumbleweeds is "more trouble than it's worth; time to turn around." When I did, I found something even more interesting—a place where a small spring was flowing out of a wall. This was, I thought, a slot canyon being born, the spring a birth canal where rainwater, percolating down through the sandstone, fought its inexorable way to sea level. In another ten thousand, hundred thousand, or ten million years, it would have nothing but daylight above it.

Where the rock opened up, there was an alluvial fan of saturated clay, maybe ten feet across. I stuck my finger in it, and I felt suction when I pulled my finger out. The clay, with its suspension of microscopic particulates, was more like paint than mud. When I stuck my foot in it, the suction nearly pulled my boot off. The consistency or viscosity was something like the cornstarch colloids kids sometimes make in elementary school science classes. I wondered if I'd discovered a patch of the legendary quicksand you'd sometimes see depicted in westerns and Tarzan movies. I picked up a rock, about the size of a football, and chucked it into the middle of the alluvial fan. The surface seemed to hold the rock at first, as a crown-shaped shockwave ringed the point of impact in slow motion, almost like the time-lapse videos of water droplets splashing into a pool below. I wondered how deep this pool of quicksand was, but there was no way to find out short of jumping directly into it. I'd seen those westerns and Tarzan movies and knew there was no future in it.

I sat for a few moments, downing a Clif Bar and a bottle of water and listening, in the stark quietude, to miniature landslides all around me, sand slides where, somewhere high above me, a field mouse or a passing centipede kicked loose a single grain of sand, and that single grain fell into two grains, which knocked into four like billiard balls increasing in number exponentially until gravity ultimately built a slope of scree at the bottom of the canyon. I thought of a video I saw once called "Powers of Ten," which starts with a couple of Chicagoans having a picnic on the shores of Lake Michigan, then zooms out to infinity, then zooms back in to infinity as the telescope turns into a microscope.

I decided it was time to head back.

I reversed my direction and walked until I arrived at the clot of tumbleweeds. I felt a sinking sensation, because it meant I'd missed the turn I needed to take. The problem with exploring slot canyons is that you don't have a bird's eye view, and you're the mouse in the maze surrounded by walls, and unless you do something to mark the way you came, you can have trouble finding your way out. Unless you kept turning around to memorize the path back, there are basically two separate canyons: the one you saw going in and the one you see going out, and they're not the same. The usual way for a hiker to mark his trail is to build cairns, small piles of stones stacked vertically with the largest on the bottom and the smallest on the top. You can even arrange your cairns sequentially where your first turn has one rock atop the base, your second turn has two, your third has three, and so on, so that when you reverse directions you can count down and know how much farther you need to go. Some of the simplest mistakes are made in haste.

I was, in short, lost, because I hadn't built any cairns and I knew I wasn't in Canyon A, or Canyon B, but I wasn't quite sure if I was in C, D, E, or F. Trying to follow my own footprints wasn't going to help because I hadn't left any on the slick rock and I couldn't tell my footprints apart from all the other indentations in the sand I'd crossed through. Plus, there wasn't any mud, which might have given me the information I needed. If I couldn't find my pack and the rope I'd left in place, I wasn't going anywhere. More to my chagrin, I'd taken the day and made the decision to venture off so casually (or perhaps because I was distracted by my worry about the dog) that I hadn't called Michelle to tell her where I was going or to give her a drop dead time. I was alone.

I reversed direction again and walked slowly, studying the rock walls for anything that looked familiar, even though after a while, everything looks the same and your vision starts to swim and you can zone out. Each twist and turn reveals another twist and turn, and you can't remember if you need to turn left or right.

I started once again feeling like I'd walked too far. I was hoping to see something that looked familiar, but everything looked familiar, and nothing did. How would I know if what I was seeing was familiar from the first time through or from this instant, as I passed it a second time? I grew more than a little concerned.

I decided to slow down and think carefully and not panic. Even if I hadn't given Michelle a drop dead time, sooner or later she'd realize it was unlike me to not check in with her. She'd call someone. That someone would call someone else, and somebody would report finding my truck and deduce where to search from where I left it, and everything was going to be okay. That was generally how things had gone in my life once Michelle entered it. As much as I enjoyed being a lone wolf, she was what made everything okay.

We first "met" via a letter. My dad and her mom knew each other and, as proud parents often do, they thought it would be wonderful to get us together. One day I received a letter from her—nothing special, just a brief introduction and pleasantries. She didn't know me and was probably just humoring her mother. She had also recently ended a relationship and wasn't exactly eager to jump right into a new one, especially with a "worldly guy." I say that because she was, at the time, a practicing Jehovah's Witness, though I didn't know that then.

I decided to write her back, inquisitively asking about her boat care business, where she lived (Florida), what it was like living on a boat, that sort of thing—just small talk. But the small talk kept growing. After we exchanged a couple of letters, I let her know I was going to Florida in January to visit my grandparents in St. Petersburg. I asked if there was any chance of us getting together. She liked the idea, but couldn't make any promises.

As it turned out, we weren't able to meet in person, but we did spend almost four hours on the phone one night. The ease of communication was remarkable, as was the sense that we understood each other and shared many views and beliefs. There was obviously something between us.

My first impression of Michelle was that she struck me as being very driven and hardworking. She owned her own boat care business, which I respected, given that I wanted to own my own construction businesses. I also noticed a couple of subtle things about her. For one, she never cursed. In the Marines, I had a sergeant who once dropped the F-bomb forty-six times in a seven-minute class he was teaching. (We actually counted.) The fact that I hadn't heard a single cuss word in nearly four hours of talking to Michelle was strikingly apparent.

She also had a sweetness, and an innocence, that I had never witnessed in anyone else. It was so disarming.

After my trip to Florida, we routinely exchanged letters or called each other, usually talking two to three times a week. Our conversations steadily lengthened, until one night we had a marathon eight-hour conversation, sweaty ears and all. It became apparent that not only did we enjoy each other's company, but we needed each other, needed someone with whom we could share our thoughts.

Somewhere around our third or fourth call, she shared something deeply personal with me. Some folks in her church were really making her life hard. They were very judgmental and controlling and she was suffering pretty nasty stomachaches and headaches because of their treatment. I'm no poet, but I decided to write her something short to help her feel better. There was a line in it that said something like, "Because someone far away loves you . . ." It felt like a pretty bold move, but it was what I was starting to feel. It felt appropriate, at that stage in our relationship, to use those words. Not only did she catch that line, but she brought it up to me later. She said it gave her "butterflies."

I wrote her back, saying I'd be interested in getting together in person.

We finally met in person in April 1998. The anticipation was off-the-hook extraordinary. She had to pull off an escape from Indiantown, Florida, where she lived on her father's boat. Her family, like mine, rarely dealt with problems or issues head-on (one of the many things we had in common). Her father knew she'd been speaking with me on the phone—and that I was not a Jehovah's Witness—but he had yet to confront her about me. Somehow, he discovered she was flying to southern California to visit me for a long weekend. She found out later he was on his way to speak with her the morning she left, and in fact, she would have run into him on his way to the marina to talk to her if she hadn't taken a different route.

She flew into John Wayne Airport in Orange County on a Thursday evening. We'd never actually seen each other, so we wore specific outfits for easy identification. I recognized her instantly from a photo she'd sent me. Her height—five feet, even—also made her fairly recognizable. We hugged and exchanged awkward but excited glances.

That night, we went to Balboa peninsula in Newport Beach and had our first real face-to-face conversation. It was pure magic. I was finally seeing someone I'd shared so much with, and she felt the same way. We talked about her situation with the elders in her congregation and the hypocrisy they were showing toward her, but at the same time, she felt guilty, questioning the things she'd been raised to believe. She was dealing with her own serious struggles, as was I, but we quickly found a sort of salvation and safe harbor in each other. It's the reason we fell for each other so quickly. We had our first kiss on the wall next to Newport Pier.

I like to think that the first time Michelle saved me was during that meeting, and that it's the best thing that ever happened to me. All the other things I thought would change my life up until that point had ended in disappointment. I'd learned, early on, that I'd never be a Navy SEAL because candidates cannot have vision worse than 20/200 correctable to 20/20. Mine was 20/400, which was a deal breaker, and there was nothing I could do (no ocular exercises) that could change that. I became a Marine instead, but that was a mixed bag. Some of my greatest memories took place during my service, and I absolutely transitioned into adulthood in a way no other experience could have given me, but it disappointed, too, because the Marines was not a good career choice for me. There was too much entrenched intractable thinking, based on nothing more than tradition, where I was constantly told, "We've done it this way forever, and we're going to continue to do it this way forever." It was also my first real exposure to politics. I watched a high school dropout get promoted over me because he could polish his boots to a shine and answer irrelevant questions about Marine history and customs. I could out-shoot him in the range and best him in any physical challenge he could name, but it didn't matter. It soured my attitude. It was the idea of moving in and settling down with Michelle that got me through the last few months of my military service.

I soon realized she was my opposite in many ways. Where I push, she glides. She's quick to pick up new technologies—I like mechanical challenges, but learning a new computer program isn't something I'm good at. She is, though. I'm good at linear convergent thinking, where she's good at non-linear creative thinking and coming up with outside-the-box solutions to problems. I'm good at math, but she does the books in our businesses. She's sociable and personable, maybe because she grew up with three half-siblings from her father's second marriage, though they were so much younger than her. She had problems with her stepmother similar to the problems I had with mine, but not to the same extent. She more or less helped raise her siblings and, in doing so, developed the psychological resilience psychologists say helps people survive and prevail. She was a caretaker then, just like she is now.

Her father owned a car dealership but spent his winters on a boat in the Bahamas, so Michelle grew up around boats and boat people. When they were in the Bahamas, she and her father lived on his boat, fished for food, traded services for the things they needed, and took showers in the rain. She was still a teenager when she started her own business, more or less babysitting boats, clearing clogged scuppers so that the rain could drain from the decks, charging the batteries, pumping out the bilges, and doing basic maintenance on boats when the owners weren't using them. She grew up to be an incredibly hard worker and extremely competent, and I know that when you're trying to describe a romantic relationship, "hardworking" and "competent" may not be the first things most people would think of to explain compatibility, but we recognized these things in each other when we met. We impressed each other, and we respected and admired each other. I'm not sure how you could love someone without being impressed by them and respecting them.

We decided that after I got out of the Marines, and after a summer working construction in Costa Mesa first to raise some cash, I'd move to Newport, Rhode Island, where she was crewing aboard a seventy-eight-foot schooner named *Adirondack*. I got lucky and found a job as First Mate aboard a sixty-eight-foot antique sail-boat, *Gleam*, built in 1937. Having no sailing experience, I did what I'd learned to do as a Marine: improvise and adapt. It was a rewarding experience, but I found myself in familiar territory after the guests debarked and the boat was tidied up, and I didn't feel welcome socializing with the crew. The wiring from my past, the instinct to hold myself apart until I was sure what was going on, was harming me instead of protecting me.

In October of '98 we moved to St. Thomas, which is part of the U.S. Virgin Islands, along with St. John and St. Croix. It's the only place in the United States territories where everybody drives on the left side of the road, but the cars they drive are imported from the United States, so they all have the steering wheels on the left side of the car instead of on the right, the way they do in England. It was soon apparent that St. Thomas was a very nice place to visit or vacation, but it wasn't a good place for me to live. I felt something like those cars, a misfit, built for somewhere else. I was a jarhead fresh out of the uniform, where I'd trained to shoot guns and kill people and, in a general sense, to be antisocial in the most lethal way possible. In St. Thomas, I got a job working as a crew member/bartender on a tour boat, serving drinks and making gourmet meals for charter guests. I thought the best way to transition out of the military would be to do something completely different, but I was wrong; to say I had an identity crisis is an understatement.

The boat I worked on was a day-trip charter that ran the same route, day after day after day, which made the job of bartending and cooking food even more mundane and repetitive than it already was. Michelle, who was more accustomed to marina culture than I, worked on a party boat that went different places and celebrated different occasions with a more interesting clientele who paid better and left her massive tips. She was having a ball, while I was being told by my boss to think of more fun ways to cut up and display pineapples. Even for someone with a mechanical or engineering mind, there are only so many fun ways to cut up a pineapple. Michelle and I saw each other only occasionally, when our schedules were somehow in sync. If she was working, I spent my down time riding my mountain bike all over the island or climbing the rocks.

I'd gone from feeling useful, doing a dangerous and important job with geopolitical ramifications, and feeling mentally and physically challenged every day, to cutting pineapples for yutzes in a tropical hospitality industry, surrounded by people whose goal in life was to not do anything, ever. Half the population of St. Thomas was on welfare or worked for the government, and the other half was on vacation. Some of the boating crowd had worked hard before retiring, it's true, I knew that, but I couldn't sympathize with the inclination toward laziness. If you work hard and make a lot of money, good for you, spend it on whatever you want, but if you make a lot of money and then just quit being useful to anybody else, what was the point? The point, for me, was that I was miserable in paradise.

One of the few reprieves from my general unhappiness in the Caribbean occurred the evening I proposed to Michelle. I'd secured a small powerboat from my boss, got a day off from crewing the sunset charter, and told Michelle to meet me at the dock as soon as she got off work, saying I wanted to go for a boat ride. A few weeks earlier, I'd gone to St. John and had a custom ring designed for her, but I wanted to present it to her in the most romantic way possible. When Michelle was a little girl, her nickname was "Seashell." I found a custom jeweler and had him fashion a ring that featured his own "wave" design for the band, a dolphin holding a diamond in its belly, and a tiny seashell opposite the dolphin. It could not have been more appropriate for a girl who'd grown up sailing in the Caribbean.

As the sun set, we motored over to Honeymoon Beach on St. John. I knew the area well because we'd anchored the charter boat there every day for lunch. I dropped anchor just offshore and we swam to the beach. I'd tied the ring to the drawstring of my shorts. Michelle didn't notice that every thirty seconds or so, I fondled my waistband to make sure I hadn't lost her ring.

We walked ashore just as the first stars came out. She still thought we were simply out for an evening boat ride. I had her sit on my lap, and as we talked, I carefully undid the knot and slipped the ring into my left hand. As we looked up at the Milky Way, I took her left hand in mine and asked her if she would grow old with me, and look up at these same stars, years from now. As I spoke, I slipped the ring on her finger. She gasped, put her arms around me, and said yes. That moment is one I'll never forget, a moment we shared together. I felt loved, truly loved, at last, and I felt safe.

She was dying to see the ring better, but without any light, she had to wait till we got back to Sapphire Marina. To this day, she says it's the most beautiful ring she's ever seen. That means a lot to me. Her ring, like our relationship, is unique. Many couples share a life together, but I don't know how many really find a deep connection like we have together.

By spring, Michelle saw how miserable I was, and agreed to move back to the States. For some couples, mutually shared hardship can lead to breakups, but for us, it made us feel even closer. We moved to South Milwaukee, Wisconsin. In the fall of 1999, we got married at the Wind Point Lighthouse in Racine. We were both barefoot, and we walked down the aisle together, to the altar and back, rather than be escorted or "given away" by our parents. That was symbolically important to us both because it showed how we were then, as we've always been, each other's biggest supporters.

In the fall of 2000, having survived the dreaded Y2K, we packed all our belongings into a five-by-eight-foot open bed trailer, with room to spare, and drove west. Our destination was either Anchorage, Alaska, or Southern California. We decided we'd figure it out along the way.

We chose to return to Southern California and settled in Dana Point. Michelle decided her dream job was to sell yachts out of the harbor. I was uncertain whether she could pull it off, but I wished her luck as she headed to the harbor to knock on doors. I should never have doubted her. She was hired on the spot and, within three months, became the top sales agent.

I found work in the harbor as a Marine technician, working for a young entrepreneurial guy who owned an outfitting/commissioning company. Michelle sold boats and I worked on them. This lasted for just under two years. We befriended a successful businessman who later backed us in purchasing Dream Catcher Yachts, the brokerage where Michelle worked.

I learned there are basically two kinds of people who buy yachts— those who know what they're doing and are going to have fun on their yachts, and those who think they know what they're doing and are going to try their best to kill themselves, or come close. It's a little bit like selling motorcycles, where guys come into the dealership and say, "That looks like fun—I want to try it." Men who buy motorcycles are, according to statistics, most likely to have an accident within the first six months of ownership, within ten miles of home, and the consequences of mental slips or mechanical failures are often dire. I learned that the hard way in Wisconsin, prior to joining Michelle in Newport, when my motorcycle literally exploded into hundreds of pieces after I hit the curb on a freeway on-ramp and went airborne. I was lucky and suffered only a sprained ankle.

I had called a friend to come pick me up. His mother knew my father and called Mark to tell him what had happened. My friend's mother gave me a big hug when she saw me and appreciated the fact that I was still shaken up from the accident. When my father arrived, he said only, "There's the asshole." He wasn't making a joke. He proceeded to scold me for not wearing a helmet. This was how he handled emotions that made him uncomfortable. First, he would put on his strong-man tough-guy demeanor and scold. Only later, after he'd calmed down, did he give me a hug and say he was glad I was alright.

That said, at least guys who buy motorcycles have some familiarity with how highways work, what other cars are likely to do, and how weather conditions can change or affect the roads. Many of the yacht buyers I encountered were men who'd suddenly found themselves with large amounts of money to spend, men who'd said, "That looks like fun—I want to try it," and bought a million-dollar boat without any marine experience or awareness whatsoever. They'd head out to sea, thinking, "How hard could it be?" Then they'd see Catalina Island on the horizon, thirty-five miles off Dana Point, and think, "I can sail there, no problem." I'd try to tell them that the Catalina Channel, which is 1,500 feet deep, is just as dangerous as being in the middle of the open ocean, but that seldom convinced them. The ocean is not always a safe environment. The consequences for making mistakes are greater on the ocean than they are riding a motorcycle.

Oftentimes I was asked to take them for a test drive in the harbor to show them how things worked, especially coming into and leaving the dock. I'd get the boat out from the slip and turn the steering wheel over to them and I'd see their stress levels go up and up, until they'd panic and start to lose control of the boat, nearly crashing into the fuel or pump-out dock. I used to pilot sixty-foot motor yachts fresh off the freighter from China, boats so new they didn't have autopilots installed yet, from San Diego to Dana Point to deliver them to the buyers. A few times, I got into tough spots a mere hundred yards from shore. Currents, rocks, waves, fog—conditions can change suddenly and without warning.

The business was doing all right, just as a lot of businesses were doing all right, until the crash of 2008 when the economic bubble derived from mortgage-based securities burst. Anyone who spent any time on Craigslist or eBay in 2008 knows that the first thing that happens when the economy crashes is that boys sell their toys, things like boats or motorcycles. Suddenly, everyone was selling his yacht, or trying to, though no one was buying.

Fine, my wife Michelle and I thought. *We're intelligent resourceful people. We can roll with the times.* We came up with what we thought was a surefire business plan. In a failing economy, we figured, people who can no longer afford to pay other people to solve their problems become do-it-yourselfers. When I served in the Marines, I became acquainted with the idea of a hobby shop, a self-service garage equipped with tools and hoists where Marines could work on their own cars. It seemed like a no-brainer—the idea could work in the civilian world. We liquidated our boat inventory, sold the business, and, after calculating that Salt Lake City was full of frugal do-it-yourselfers, moved there to open a shop called the Wrench-It Center. We weren't wrong about Salt Lake residents, but it was still a struggle.

After one year, the business was still in the red. Michelle and I were working twelve- and fourteen-hour days, and we were under constant financial stress, postponing bill payments and unable to repay a good friend who'd invested in the business by loaning us the startup costs. Worse than that, the business itself was growing in the wrong direction. We'd initially offered, for an extra fee, the services of an on-site consulting mechanic, and that part of the business was booming, but it was turning the self-service shop into a hybrid assisted-service garage, which was never the original idea. Now there were too many people, wanting too many things, having too many conflicts in need of mediation or resolution.

"It's going to be all right," Michelle told me.

I reflected on these thoughts and memories, among others, as searched the tributary canyons, looking for my backpack. Michelle had rescued me from the Marines, from the Virgin Islands, and in many ways from the falling out I had with my father. And she was going to be at my side now, with the Wrench-It Center, come what may, and with the dog.

Part of being bullied is growing up believing you won't ever be loved. It can seem only logical, because if it's so hard to simply be liked, being *loved* can seem as impossible and out of reach as walking on the moon. Some kids, of course, console themselves knowing that at least their mother and/or their father loves them. For reasons I couldn't understand, I never had that either. Then Michelle found me, and then I was walking on the moon.

A moment later, I saw the weathered deflated soccer ball, and I knew where I was. That was all I needed—a sign that I was headed in the right direction.

I received a sign that the puppy was headed in the right direction when I returned to the animal hospital, around three that afternoon. I immediately noticed something different: there was a small cup of dry dog food next to the cage door that he'd been eating from.

Krista said he was still in rough shape, and couldn't be expected to function normally yet, but he was on the mend. She was capable and professional, and perhaps a bit inured to the anguish I was feeling, but there probably wasn't any way for her to do her job if she didn't learn to distance herself. All doctor and nurses lose patients, I knew. I wondered if the statistics were higher for veterinarians, whose patients are unable to report their maladies and miseries.

I opened the door and put a piece of dog food by his mouth. Without raising his head, he opened his mouth and gulped it down. I fed him the whole cup. They told me to feed him as much as he'd eat, so I poured more in and fed him an entire second cup.

On my way out the door, I saw the cat I'd seen Dr. Roundtree treating earlier in the day. It wasn't moving, but I assumed it was still hanging on, because if it wasn't, they would have moved it somewhere.

The cat set me on a darker path. I thought again of what kind of person might have put the dog in the slot canyon where I found him. I came up with one possible answer.

7

In one way, I was lucky. I was a kid just before the digital age, which introduced a new era and a whole new way of bullying. In my day, I was afraid I'd see my name written on the wall in the boys' room at school. Today, kids get picked on in places like Facebook or Foursquare, Twitter, Instagram, and things are written on virtual walls. There's no way to erase the hurtful comments, the names, the insults, and the verbal aggression if they don't have control of the page. On the Internet, hurtful comments get copied and pasted and reposted and go viral, and the victim has no recourse whatsoever. The verbal harassment is more anonymous than ever before. I assume that if someone from another country sees an unflattering picture of a kid who's being bullied, they might feel free (and why not—who will ever know?) to add a hateful and hate-filled comment beneath the photograph. Now, when some poor kid feels like the whole world is against him, he's not being metaphorical.

The solution to bullying, experts will tell you, now and when I was a kid, is empathy. For me, though, it was lifting weights and learning how to literally make myself stronger. In doing so,

I learned to respect myself in a way I never had before, and once I respected myself, and really started to know who I was, the kids who'd bullied me stopped. They didn't necessarily turn around and instantly become my best friends, nor did I want them to, but they stopped bothering me, which was all that really mattered.

I can't say I could point to any particular individual who learned empathy and stopped bullying. They stopped not because they realized I had feelings, but because they sensed continuing to bully me would come at a cost. If Leona or Ben or Matt or Scott or Joey or any of them tried to hurt me or humiliate me, with my new body and my new self-respect, I would have retaliated and then, just as Mrs. Kulba had predicted, even if I lost the fight—and I didn't think I would—the game would be over, because it wouldn't be a game anymore. They would realize I had feelings, and that I could make them feel, too.

The irony is that as much as I tried to make myself invisible, and I succeeded insofar as I was invisible to them—they did not recognize that I had feelings, or rather they could not empathize with what I was feeling. That is to say, they were afraid to. There's a line in the movie *Casablanca* where Ugarte, the character played by Peter Lorre, says to Rick Blaine, played by Humphrey Bogart, "You hate me, don't you?" Bogart replies, "I probably would if I gave it any thought." I read a story in a magazine, or maybe it was a newspaper, in which a man, now grown, arranges a meeting with another man who had bullied him mercilessly when they both were kids, but the ex-bully (if ex-bullies can truly be said to exist) didn't remember it that way, couldn't recall being mean, and hadn't really given it any thought. I was invisible to my tormentors in that they never really considered me, didn't really know what they were doing, or—more to the point—didn't care, because they never put themselves in my shoes.

If there's hope, it's in the belief sociologists and psychologists have that empathy can be taught. I am not so sure. I mean, yes, perhaps it can be taught, but the thing that makes psychopaths pathological is their inability to feel or empathize, and if it's not there . . . it's just not there. They are not going to suddenly start growing a conscience and realize what they do is wrong. Perhaps a small percentage of them might, but the majority are themselves damaged, and the damage is unlikely to be undone.

Cruelty to animals is one indicator FBI profilers look at when they're trying to parse the motivations and origins of criminal personalities. According to the ASPCA website, various reports and surveys suggest that anywhere from 70 to 90 percent of battered women seeking protection in women's shelters report that their abusive partners were also abusive to the women's pets and companion animals, and that often women stay in abusive relationships because they don't dare leave their pets behind and they know they can't take them when they seek refuge at a shelter. There's been a recent effort to get women's shelters to accept and accommodate pets for this very reason.

Leaving the Page Animal Hospital on the second night, it occurred to me that that was the only logical reason—if twisted psychopathic thinking can be said to have its own internal logic— why anyone would bother to take the puppy I'd found and rappel three times into the deepest part of an inaccessible canyon to leave it behind. They probably did it not to hurt the puppy, but to cause misery to the dog's owner. I could almost imagine the taunts that came with it, possibly even with a photograph attached:

"Look what I did to your stupid dog—I put him where nobody is ever going to find him. I want you to think of him every night as he slowly starves to death. After what you did to me, it's the least you deserve. . . ."

Or words to that effect.

Somebody, probably male, was getting even, avenging a hurt. Again, according to the ASPCA website, people who abuse animals in domestic relationships do so to "... demonstrate power and control over the family; to isolate the victim and children; to enforce submission; to perpetuate an environment of fear; to prevent the victim from leaving or coerce her to return; and to punish for leaving or showing independence." All those things might explain why someone demented and evil would go to such lengths to abandon an innocent puppy. To this person, it was not only a way to hurt a loved one, but also a way to demonstrate continuing power over her.

That might explain the question as to why someone did it, but when I left the animal and went to check into the Motel 6 again for one more night, I was thinking more about the cat I saw than the dog, because the cat triggered another memory—another time when I was probably feeling as lost as I'd ever felt, even more than when suicide seemed a viable option.

One day after school, I'm sitting in the rocking chair, watching television, and I notice that the cat's tail is under the front arc of the rocker, so I rock forward, causing the cat to screech in pain and bolt for the next room. Part of me feels a rush of energy, a feeling of power, though the cat had never done anything to me. I did it only to see what would happen. I justify it by telling myself it wasn't as if I'd hurt another human being, another sentient creature who deserved to be treated with respect, as an equal—it's just a cat.

The worst abuse comes one night when I'm lying in bed with one of the cats lying on the bed with me. It begins accidentally, when I move and the cat falls into the space between the mattress and the wall. The cat is momentarily stuck and manages to extract herself by digging in her claws and pulling herself up. It is a bit of an ordeal for her, but she survives, no worse for wear, panting, her tongue out. I idly wonder what would happen if I do it again. It's almost like an experiment. If she could get out of a space that tight, what will happen if the space is even tighter? I don't hate the cat. I actually like this cat. I'm not being malicious. I'm curious. I just want to see what will happen. The cat's feelings don't enter into it; I don't stop to consider the possibility that she has any. I hook the cat by the collar and jam her back into the space between the mattress and the wall, but this time, I push against the mattress to make her escape more difficult. After considerable struggle, she pulls herself out, trembling and so scared that she defecates on the bed.

In an instant, I realize what I've done was wrong.

I stop, horrified. Now I'm scared, as if something monstrous inside me has made me do something I didn't want to do. I hold the cat and stroke it and try to undo any damage I might have inflicted, and after a few seconds, the cat takes me back, so it seems, and returns the affection.

This is the worst of it. I am confused and troubled by the fact that I have knowingly tormented my mom's cats, in this terribly difficult period in my youth. I have become as bad as those kids who've tormented me—it's as though I have been infected by whatever malevolent force drives them to torment me.

As pathetic as it was, dominating those cats was a means of affirming that I was not always the victim; I could be in control of something. I had power over them, and having power over them proved I had power, which, when you feel so powerless in every other way, affirms something. I failed to realize, before I did it, that it meant I would be guilty of the same sort of behaviors I faulted others for, and that was a sign of my immaturity, but it also took a long time for me to realize I was a person of value, a worthwhile human being in my own right. That I was better than that. A bullied kid can start believing the things people say about him.

I've also read that the frontal lobes in teenage boys, the part of the brain that controls impulses, is late to develop, and that sometimes teenage boys do things and honestly don't know why they did them. They really can't perform the prognostic computations that would let them foresee the consequences of their actions. I wasn't thinking, but that's exactly the point.

Lying in bed in the Motel 6, not tired enough to turn out the lights, I felt the guilt I still carry about mistreating my mom's cats, but in a way, that's what kids do—kids push to find the boundaries of their lives, and since there was no one to set boundaries for me, I set my own and learned, the hard way, what it meant to go too far. I had a sudden attack of empathy, as if I'd temporarily forgotten myself and then remembered, but I could see how other kids might not have the same revelation. That is perhaps the other side of bullying: victims turn around and become bullies themselves, thinking that inflicting abuse can ease their own in a self-perpetuating vicious cycle, or cycle of viciousness, where the powerless, fearful of their own weakness, lash out at people who seem even less powerful. This moves on down the social ladder, extending even to the dogs and cats and animals that live with us, which we assail in proxy, symbolically hurting not them, but what they stand for or represent.

My best guess, then, as to who put the dog in the canyon was that he was a male who had felt powerless as a child, and who had tormented animals at a young age but never had understood that animals are sentient creatures that, to some extent, experience the same fears and emotions we do. He was probably someone who felt isolated and alone and hurt as a kid and who had learned that hurting something else made him feel better. As despicable as the act was, it seemed reasonable to speculate that whoever did it was himself the product of a dysfunctional, abusive childhood. I supposed that if a good police detective were interested in canvasing the neighboring towns and ranches, he might have been able to figure out if there were any battered women, and if they'd reported pets missing, but then there was a chance the dog would be returned to the abusive environment it first came from, and that wasn't going to happen.

If I could, I would have said to the abuser, "Something went wrong for you. I'm sure putting this dog in the pothole wasn't the first time you hurt an animal. Your wife or your girlfriend hurt you, so you wanted to hurt her back in the most vicious way possible, and you thought you got away with it. You never considered what the dog might have been feeling, so let me paint a picture for you. When you climbed up out of the pothole and looked down as you were pulling the rope up behind you, he was probably staring up at you, wagging his tail, wondering what was next. After you left, he probably kept staring at the place where he last saw you. Kept hoping you'd come back. Eventually, he lay down to wait. When he was thirsty, he drank from the water at the bottom of the hole, but as he got hungrier and hungrier, he began to whimper, maybe even bark a little, even though he knew no one could hear him. Eventually, he lay down and waited for the end to come. You live in a world of payback and retribution, a world where you think nobody is going to mess with you because if they do, you're going to mess with them. If that's your idea of strength, it's really your prison, just as surely as the pothole you left the dog in was his."

Now I had what I believed could be answers to the why and the who, but as I considered the idea that bullying was a kind of legacy—something passed from person to person and down the generations, like a disease that was both contagious and hereditary—I started thinking about the central question of my childhood, a question that had remained unanswered into my adult life: Why me? Why was I bullied? What was it about me that singled me out?

If you do a little research into bullying, you'll find it described in terms of animal behavior where, in most species that live in communities or aggregations, the forces of dominance and subordination determine a social order, an order that isn't set but shifts as its members grow and change with age. There's a pecking order among chickens that determines who gets to eat first. There's a bunting order among cattle, set as they knock into each other to see who gets to the feed trough first. Packs of wolves and prides of lions have alpha males and alpha females who dominate the group and call all the shots. In all these groups, in herds of wild stallions and on beaches full of walruses or elephant seals, an aggressive male will occasionally challenge the alpha male and make him defend his position. It's the stuff of nearly every nature show I'd ever seen on television, the footage of rams butting horns or grizzlies baring their teeth to each other.

I'd never, to my knowledge, overtly challenged any of the dominant boys in my classes, but I did present to them an opportunity to safely display their power and assert their dominance without any risk. Bullies often learn to be bullies at home, and have parents who display anger or are verbally aggressive toward each other or toward their kids. Bullies learn that behavior at home and take it to school, where they apply it to gain social status or power, but they don't bully kids who look like they're going to fight back, because they would risk losing power, not gaining or maintaining it. They don't pick on kids who have large groups of friends who will back them up. They identify loners, and then they isolate the loners by labeling them as losers, as people no one would want to be friends with. You can hear it in conversations that can seem subtle and indirect, the cool bully girl at the mall who says to her sidekick in disbelief, "Eeeuuw—you're friends with *her*?" In tone and inflection, the message is clear—nobody should be friends with *her*. And then the next time the three are together, the sidekick snubs *her* to show the cool girl whose side she's on, and *her* is blindsided and doesn't know what just happened. Bullies only pick on kids it's safe to pick on, kids who don't know what to do or how to react, and all they want is to avoid or escape the negative comments and hurtful judgments, so they try to be invisible. They try to *not do* whatever it is that's inviting attacks, unaware that it's exactly their passivity, their *not doing* anything, that makes them such easy targets. Bullies are motivated by fear, fear of losing status and of being weak or isolated or excluded, so they attack to protect something they're afraid of losing. They choose victims who pose the least threat, the ugly girl or the developmentally challenged boy whose parents are trying to mainstream him.

And more often than not, they don't see what they're doing. They don't see themselves. That might have been the biggest disconnect of all, because I was, as a kid, supremely self-conscious and aware of every move I made and every step I took, constantly scrutinizing my own behavior, to identify and avoid doing whatever it was that I was doing wrong and getting bullied for, while at the same time scanning the horizon for signs of trouble, all my sensors and bully detectors set at maximum. It was true that I wasn't aware of how my passivity and avoidance behaviors were inviting the trouble I was trying to escape, but I was aware of what I did. I don't know if there's a measurable percentage that could ever be obtained, where you could get a thousand bullies in a room and give them all a test and say 35 percent of them knew they were being bullies and 65 percent did not, but I would bet money that the majority, probably the large majority, do not think they're doing anything wrong. If they see bullying at home, or if they're bullied by their parents, when they get to school and in turn bully a schoolmate, it's just normal to them. They might also think it's all relative, the star athlete who wins a championship for his high school, and maybe gets good grades too, so if he's mean to some kid he considers a twerp, his achievements and finer attributes more than balance it all out. Bullies learn at home not just how to bully but how to hide it, from others and from themselves.

You would suppose that with our larger brains, our capacity for altruism, our ability to see things in ethical and moral terms, our sense of mortality and final judgment, our belief that we all have souls—our conviction that we are more highly evolved that chickens or cows or horses or bears or elephant seals—that we might have transcended the struggle for dominance by now, but that did not seem to be the case. Instead, I thought, we'd passed on the worst part of our natures, from one generation to the next.

It occurred to me, then, that if being a bully was something learned at home, perhaps being a victim was, too. I grew up angry at my father and my mother for not protecting me or teaching me how to protect myself. My father, when I was with him, either bullied me or allowed Robin to. He either looked the other way or wasn't there.

It was my mother who I spent most of my time with—so why didn't she teach me how to stand up for myself or protect myself?

The answer was simple. She couldn't teach me how to do something she couldn't do herself, any more than I could teach someone how to knit or fly an airplane. She could only teach me the lessons she'd learned.

She could not have meant to, but in a sense, my mother prepared me for a period, if not a life, of victimization simply because she was victimized at nearly every stage of her life. I'd seen how she sabotaged herself, making herself late for everything, her way of making herself a victim before anyone else could, similar to how the victims of bullies make self-deprecating jokes and, for example, call themselves fat before anybody else can. Part of being a victim is lacking basic problem-solving skills, not understanding what people wanted and never learning how to negotiate with them.

Getting to work on time is important. Being late all the time is a problem. No one can argue it isn't a problem, but it's one anybody can solve. You get an alarm clock. You set it. But she couldn't do it.

I'd seen how she exhibited obsessive compulsive behaviors, like cleaning the sink or the stove, as if she didn't know what else to do to be a mother. As if a clean stove or a clean sink were the only things she knew she could do to be proud of herself for achieving something that was, in her mind, significant, and that was all she saw. The rest of the kitchen could be a mess, but the stove was clean, so she'd fulfilled an obligation. She was self-absorbed because it was her way of minding her own business and keeping her head down, the same way I was when I was eating lunch in the cafeteria, shielding myself from hurt by not making eye contact with anybody. She'd modeled the behavior, and I'd copied it.

I was far too young to remember anything about the time when she and my father were married. I do have faint memories of them interacting, albeit awkwardly. I must have been five. My dad dropped me off at my home in Cudahy early in the morning on his way to work. He came upstairs a few times and I witnessed something that didn't make sense, because I was too small. My mother was lying on the couch, where she would often sleep. Mark sat down next to her and taunted and teased her, tickling her. Her words said stop, but her tone said she liked the attention. She even asked me to help her, a ridiculous thing to say, as if a five-year-old could physically stop his dad from grab-assing with his mom. I remember feeling a plethora of confusing emotions, from helpless to angry to confused. Was this normal? Was this what parents did? How was I to know any different? It was all just too much for me to process.

But to understand someone, of course, you need to look at where you've come from and what forces shaped them. When I did that, it became easier to understand how she could be both so timid and subordinate when she felt she was in a position of weakness, and so mean spirited and controlling when she felt the need to push me around. She was like a mouse who'd grown up in a household of cats.

She was raised in a house in Milwaukee where she lived with her brother, Sean, her mother, Alice Simon, and her father, Roland Simon, but her paternal grandparents lived downstairs in the same house. Her paternal grandmother could be a nasty old lady, a mean small-minded person who would call the police when the neighborhood kids cut through the yard, unaware that the neighborhood kids, to retaliate, would beat up my mother.

There was no love on display, ever, between her mother and father, who bickered and fought constantly and never hugged or kissed, not each other, and not her. She was constantly punished and told she was bad, a label she ultimately accepted, until she thought of herself as a bad person, a person of little value or worth. Cruelty and negative reinforcement were everywhere, every day, a constant. Praise was nonexistent. When Sandra got A's on her report card, Alice wouldn't look at it. When there was a mother-daughter function at school, Alice would not attend. She sometimes used what was once called a "switch" to administer corporal punishment for minor offenses, a believer in the old parenting adage, "Spare the rod, spoil the child." My mother shared with Michelle a story where she recalled a hot summer day when Alice bought a group of children ice cream cones, but she would not buy a cone for Sandra, who was told she was being punished and deprived of ice cream because she'd been bad. Even if being deprived of ice cream was a suitable punishment, why would Alice go the extra mile and buy all the other kids ice cream, just to make Sandra feel even worse than she already did? In high school, when my mother modeled a dress for her mother before a school dance, proudly twirling in the belief that she had successfully prettied herself up, Alice said, "You look ugly."

It was, unfortunately, not the last time she'd hear that. When I was in third or fourth grade, I became aware that she was trying a dating service called Unique Encounters, which at the time, before the Internet, meant arranging telephone conversations with potential dates or partners. She would do alright until they asked her to send them a picture. One man in particular seemed particularly enthusiastic and kept begging her to send a picture so that he could see what she looked like. When she finally complied, he stopped taking her calls and he never called her back again.

Such are the stories she told me and Michelle. I assume they're accurate, but I wonder how much she remembers, and I wonder what she might not be saying.

My grandfather, Roland, was of German descent, raised on Pierce Street in Milwaukee, the son of a man who worked for the city. I remember hearing that his father had been an amateur boxer. I don't know what my grandfather did before he joined the army air corps out of high school during World War II and served in India.

When he came home from the war, he was sent by the military to Woods Hospital, a psychiatric facility, where he was diagnosed as schizophrenic and treated with shock therapy. My mother and her mother would visit him there, and he would occasionally come home on weekends. He scored high on the intelligence tests they gave him, but he never fully recovered from the illness, which he claimed he'd come down with in the military. I wasn't sure if it actually worked that way, where schizophrenia is a contagious disease you "come down with," like the flu or chicken pox, but I knew he got disability checks from the government for the rest of his life.

My mother recalls her father as having a dual personality. She may have preferred the drunk one to the sober one, because the only time he ever told her he loved her was when he was drunk, though she didn't believe it and felt it was the alcohol talking. If she and her father were close when she was younger, it deteriorated as she grew older. Once when they fought, Roland threatened to send her away to a home for girls run by nuns. Only a freshman in high school, she believed this to be a real place. She wrote her father a long letter and put it on his pillow. He never sent her to the home run by nuns, but he never removed the threat either.

Schizophrenic is a pretty big word for a kid to understand. As a child, I believed this was something he'd contracted during his service in India with the army air corps. I thought it was something he had and got over. It didn't really dawn on me that his being in and out of mental hospitals during my mother's youth meant he had an ongoing problem. I saw for myself, on the many occasions that I would visit their house, that when my grandfather was home, he drank to excess, and then he became surly and abusive.

The worst memory I have of such an episode was when I was very young, six or seven. My grandparents got into another one of their fights, but this time the hostilities erupted rather than dissipated as they carried their argument from the living room into the kitchen and then into the bathroom, where things got physical. I heard, above the screaming, the sound of my grandmother being pushed against the wall. She yelled at him to stop pushing her. That's when I got scared. I snapped, walked into the kitchen, shaking, and screamed at them, "STOP IT!" before bursting into tears, and then I ran back into the living room and buried myself in the couch.

It worked. I'd shamed them into stopping. They sat down in the living room and actually started talking, and there was peace. I was still scared and confused by what had happened. I ran back and forth between the two of them, burying my head in their laps, one after the other, feeling sad for them, and for myself.

Because they lived only thirty minutes away, I became fairly close to Alice and Roland. I knew him as the man who built little ships and boats for me to play with out of wood scraps and found household items. I knew he was a veteran because he talked about the war, over and over again, and told me the same story about how he'd put out an engine fire on an airplane and rescued the pilot, over and over, a hundred times, until I realized one day that he talked about virtually nothing else, as if he'd spent a lifetime in the military and seen combat action, rather than the year and a half he spent working on airplanes before he was sent home. I didn't know what schizophrenia meant, other than that it was described at one time, probably at the time my grandfather was diagnosed, as having a "split personality." It means crazy, paranoid or deluded to the point of hallucinations, with unpredictable behaviors and erratic emotional responses, and an inability to function normally or think logically. People who are schizophrenic can't hold jobs, suffer from depression or anxiety disorders, and often, like my grandfather, are prone to substance abuse. Alcoholism is, in a way, its own kind of splitting, because it divides the parent into two people, the sober one and the drunk one, and little kids can never tell which one is coming at them, the sober one they can trust or the drunk one they can't.

As I said, I never saw any of this, because I was too young and it went right over my head, or because my grandfather managed to hide it from me, but my mother saw all of it. She grew up with it, and in her most formative years, it was what shaped her. It would have been difficult enough, having a crazy father, but having one who also self-medicated with alcohol made it impossible to know what to do. Sometimes the drunk one told her he loved her, but she couldn't trust the drunk one. Sometimes the drunk one pushed his wife Alice around, and when Sandra tried to come to her mother's defense, she got pushed as well. It was lucky that he was diagnosed while he was in the service, because the whole family lived off his disability checks, but it wasn't lucky for my mother.

She had no one to set a good example for her, no one to show her how to be a loving parent. As a young girl, my mother saw her mother experience a panic attack. She remembers getting on a city bus with Alice, but after only a few blocks Alice became convinced that the bus was going to crash, until eventually the driver stopped to let them out, five blocks from their stop. Alice was given a prescription for valium, one of the earlier psychotropic medications released in 1963 to treat anxiety.

My information about Alice and Roland is incomplete, because Sandra didn't like to talk about her childhood much. It was clear to me that her early life was not easy. She had nowhere to turn and no one to talk to. If she ever cried, her mother and father made fun of her for crying, rather than offer sympathy. She learned to hide, keep her head down and make herself invisible, and not to fight back.

When I was about fourteen or fifteen, she had a number of brief hospital stays, but all she'd tell me was that she had a "chemical imbalance." I've read that people who suffer from schizophrenia are hospitalized when they are considered to pose a danger to themselves or to others, which meant my mother grew up with a man who was probably diagnosed as dangerously insane. Sandra's mother and father were both, to varying degrees, mentally ill. I'm not qualified to say whether or not my mother is, too, but even if she isn't, she still grew up imitating her parents' behaviors, unconsciously. They didn't know how to show or express love, so Sandra never learned how to do it.

She has had three romantic involvements in her life, to my knowledge, and she has intimated to Michelle that her first romantic involvement with a man, before getting involved with my father, was abusive. Her first impression of Mark was that he was, I quote, "an asshole." Why, then, would she pursue a relationship with him, if not to refight the battles she'd lost as a child and, it turned out, lose them all over again? I should add that she was able to express love in one way: like many people too shy or introverted or troubled to love other human beings, she could love animals. She and my father, when they began their ill-fated marriage, had a Siberian husky named Reagan, whom my mother adored. She never forgave my father for taking the dog with him when he left. And she loved her cats—the same cats I hurt, perhaps because she loved them and not me.

The lessons I learned from my mother were the opposite of beneficial. The way I saw it, they directly resulted in my constant bullying. But how did this happen? Why was I singled out for bullying?

I once asked a therapist that. He dismissed the question and thought it was unimportant. I felt, to the contrary, that understanding what it was about me that drew the scorn and anger of my peers would be a crucial part of the healing process.

From kindergarten on, I set myself up for punishment and abuse because I'd already built a protective fortress around me, a way of carrying myself that marked me as different from everybody else. I walked on eggshells where there were no eggshells. I anticipated hostility and expected trouble, and as a result, I generated hostility and trouble. I'd learned, at home, how to behave like a victim. My peers didn't know what was different about me on any conscious level, what it was that they didn't like. It was beyond all of us. All they knew was that they didn't like it, they didn't feel comfortable around me, so they attacked what they didn't understand, afraid of becoming me.

I had "please don't victimize me" written all over me, and that invited the bullies to do as they pleased to me, knowing I wouldn't fight back, because I'd already surrendered. I did that because that's how my mother learned to cope and survive. I sabotaged myself because she'd shown me how to do it. She didn't mean to, but she did.

141

8

I returned to the Page Animal Hospital the next morning, arriving around ten o'clock. It was another bright, brilliant Arizona morning, with blue skies and a warm sun toasting the sand.

Both Krista and Dr. Roundtree were there, and I knew immediately, by the way they both smiled at me, that things had turned a corner. I was enormously impressed by how professional and caring they were. They brought me immediately to the back room. I quickly scanned the cages to see how the black-and-white cat was doing. Either he'd been moved somewhere to recover, or he hadn't made it, because I couldn't find him anywhere. But my concern was for the dog now.

"How's he doing?" I asked.

"He's still eating and taking fluids," Krista said. "We like that. And he's pooping and peeing."

"He's pretty weak," Dr. Roundtree said. "But that's to be expected."

He explained that he'd performed the same blood tests to check for organ function that he'd performed on the day I'd brought him in, which was standard procedure. You do the tests, rehydrate the dog, then do the tests again to measure the differences. As far as he could tell, the dog seemed to be bouncing back.

"Why are his teeth so brown?"

"He probably had distemper before his permanent teeth came in," Krista said. "The infection disrupts the formation of the enamel."

Krista said he was on his third I.V. bag. To put it in scale, given his size and diminished weight, it would be like a normal-sized human drinking two five-gallon jugs of water. No wonder he couldn't move. He would have sloshed himself to death. She showed me the reports of the blood work they'd done, how his electrolytes were coming back into balance, how his white cells were up, which would help him fight off infection. He was pulling through.

"So what's next?" I asked.

It wasn't a question I wanted to ask. By that, I mean that I felt responsible for the animal and wanted to pay his health-care costs. But beyond that, there was only so much I *could* do. Michelle and I had already talked about getting a second dog, and I had decided one dog was enough. We were also working long hours, seven days a week, to keep the Wrench-It Center afloat and the bills paid. Neither of us would have the time to stay home with a sick puppy and nurse him back to health. We also needed to take Kohi into consideration, and while he got along fine with other dogs, those instances were quick meet-and-greets at the park or on the street. In his own house, he was the alpha dog, and we weren't sure if he'd welcome the competition.

"Wait and see, but I think we're out of the woods."

"What about psychological damage?" I asked. "I suppose that's hard to say."

"It is," the veterinarian said. I knew the dog wouldn't be able to talk it out with a therapist, of course. There was a chance the dog would be clingy or need a lot of attention. He could show avoidant behaviors toward people, or growl, or even nip or bite. "But dogs don't think like we do. He's not going to think somebody put him in the canyon because they wanted to hurt him. They can't really tell what our motivations are."

The dog was also, I hoped, young enough that if someone was cruel to him, he might not remember, the way adult humans can't retain anything that happened to them in the first year or two of our lives.

"Do you think he'll get along with other dogs?" I asked.

"Impossible to say," I was told. "It depends on how socialized he was before he was abandoned."

"Do you think there's a chance his owner will be looking for him?"

He didn't think so. His best guess was that the dog was what they call a "res dog," referring to the Navajo reservation lands outside of Page. "Res dogs" often wandered off, looking for food. However, he didn't think anybody would have bothered putting the dog in the canyon. For one thing, few if any locals had the gear and experience to get so deep into such a technical canyon. He'd checked, but the dog didn't have any subcutaneous microchips to identify it. I wondered what the chances were that someone would adopt him. There's something called "black dog syndrome," which describes why black dogs are always the last to be adopted. What it comes down to is that people just don't like them.

The doctor left me alone with the animal. I argued with myself, even though I knew which side of the argument was going to win. It seemed like a bad idea to adopt the dog myself. Was I being overcautious? Callous? The instinct to protect myself from emotional blows was strong and entrenched. It would hurt too much if something went wrong and I brought the dog home and then he didn't make it, or turned into a major behavioral rehab project. At the same time, if I'd come this far, I couldn't stop now.

It would be like climbing all but the last ten feet of a mountain. I was afraid it would turn out to be a "false peak," which happens sometimes when you're climbing, and you think you've reached the top, and only then do you realize there's an even higher peak hiding behind the one you initially spotted.

When I knelt down next to the dog, this time he was able to lift his head from the towel I'd placed him on two days ago. When I was in the best shape of my life as a Marine, lifting weights, I'd been able to bench press 350 pounds. The dog, lifting his head from the towel, seemed to make a similar effort. His tail wagged again, this time the full tail and not just the tip, and he looked me in the eye. I think that was the moment that sealed the deal, like the moment when the first wolf pup snuck into the light of the campfire, thirty thousand years ago, and looked the first pet owner in the eye, as if to say, "You and me—Whaddaya think?"

I heard Krista approach behind me and looked up.

"Are you going home?" she asked me. "Back to Salt Lake City?"

"I do have to get back. Do you think he's ready to travel?"

She nodded.

"I can help you move him to your car and give you some extra towels for the trip," she said. It felt a bit like she was making the decision for me, but in a good way.

There was one last matter to attend to. Digging my wallet from my back pocket and then my debit card from my wallet, I went to the front desk and told the girl there that I needed to pay for the dog I'd brought in. It took her a second to print out the bill and hand it to me. I braced myself. A friend of mine had brought his dog into a veterinarian's office after it ate an oatmeal raisin cookie from Starbucks, and after they'd pumped the dog's stomach and held him overnight for observation, his bill came to almost $1,200, making it perhaps the world's most expensive raisin cookie. The dog I'd rescued was going into his third day. I wasn't sure what I'd do if his bill was anywhere near a thousand dollars a day. In desperate times, you start thinking of what you have that you can sell on eBay or Craigslist. I had plenty of room on my credit card, if I needed it, but I'm extremely conservative when it comes to money. I knew I was responsible for the poor little pup, but I struggled with the idea of spending more money than I could afford, and I felt guilty for having doubts.

The bill was a little over $600. This was what I was afraid of and had clearly not budgeted for. I looked at it and decided to see what I could do. I asked if, given the circumstances, they could please whittle it down closer to their actual costs, including labor. I didn't want to short anybody, but I simply did not have $600 to spend. It made me extremely uncomfortable even to ask for this favor; I value my integrity a lot. I told Dr. Roundtree I would own the bill, but I was hoping he could work with me on it.

Krista walked out and seemed irritated that I was looking at the bill. She took it from me and walked into the back office. A few moments later, she came back out with the invoice in her hand. Had she overheard me talking and knocked off some of the cost? Was I about to get a "pain in the ass" surcharge for trying to negotiate the bill?

Krista looked at me and said Dr. Roundtree was going to have the Angel Fund cover the bill. I asked her what the Angel Fund was. She said they tried to set aside money, when they could, to cover situations like this. The bill was going to be discounted, 100 percent. I'm guessing Dr. Roundtree had known he would use the fund to cover the pup's expenses, but I think he wanted to get some kind of a commitment out of me so that I would not just leave the dog behind. Assuming I am correct, I can completely understand this position. Charity is wonderful, but it also must subscribe to the laws of math. If they helped every animal they rescued free of charge, it would not be sustainable.

I was literally speechless; I looked at Krista and just stared.

I snapped out of it and decided negotiations were not over. I handed my card to the office manager and asked her to bill me for $200. Krista stepped in and said no.

"I'm going to contribute to the invoice," I said. "I'm extraordinarily grateful for what you have done here and I'm going to help."

She didn't go for it. Was this really going to come to blows? I'm in pretty good shape, but she was looking pretty scrappy standing there. A brief battle of wills took place, the kind I wish happened more often, and she finally gave in.

I thanked everybody for their kindness, and I shook Dr. Roundtree's hand before going outside to clean out the foot well on the passenger side of my truck, where the dog would be safer than if I allowed him to ride on the seat. They'd given the dog superb care. They'd treated and rescued hundreds of animals that had been abandoned or hit by cars or mistreated, and I had only saved one. The work they did every day was heroic, but it was new to me. A moment later, Krista came out holding the animal in both hands, her arms outstretched like a ring bearer at a wedding, the dog limp as a rag. I used the towels to make a bed for him in the foot well, and then she placed him on the bed. I felt like a new dad, coming home from the hospital with a day-old baby, a mixture of joy and dismay.

"Leave the bandage on his paw where we took out the catheter for a few days, but I don't think he'll chew it," Krista said. "Give him soft food or dry food with a little water, but in a couple of weeks I think you can give him dry food."

"I'm freaked out," I told her.

"Don't worry," she said. "You're not going to break him. Everything is going to be fine."

I closed the door. It was time to leave. I felt a very special connection to Krista in that instant, an overflowing mix of gratitude and respect. I reached out and gave her a huge hug to express my appreciation. She wished me luck.

As I drove away, I looked down at the puppy, who seemed to be sleeping. "Hope you like Salt Lake City," I told him. The words themselves meant nothing to him, I knew, but I hoped that, at the very least, the sound of my voice was comforting to him. I knew that with Kohi, when Michelle and I were doing anything at all, eating or just watching television, he needed to be in the same room. He had the run of the house and could choose to rest anywhere he wanted, but what he wanted was to be in proximity to us. I had friends with dogs who followed them everywhere they went, from room to room to room and even whimpered when the bathroom door was temporarily closed to them. Kohi was never that clingy, but all the same, he manifested the innate drive dogs have to be part of a group.

It was the same innate compulsion I had as a kid, when I felt so isolated.

As I drove north, I thought of what a therapist had told me. He thought it was possible that I'd been clinically depressed for at least the last ten years, if not longer. I'd been having serious back pain that X-rays and MRIs couldn't diagnose, and the orthopedists told me there's a school of thought that believes a certain percentage of back pain is referred, meaning the pain begins somewhere else, but you feel it in your back, and that can include emotional pain. The orthopedist sent me to a psychologist, to whom I admitted that I'd worn, since I was young, a suit of emotional armor. He told me he thought that was true, and that armor had weight, and carrying all that weight had bent me over and was causing the pain I felt in my back. He was speaking metaphorically, but that was part of his job—to give me new ways to see or think about my life and the things that were keeping me from feeling happy.

He helped me put into words many of the things that were holding me back. I didn't trust people. I was too pessimistic. My first impulse was to be cynical, until I was proven wrong. I kept people at a distance. I was overly critical of people who seemed to have it easy, people who glided through life without the same degree of effort it took me—people who had doors opened for them, when I had to knock the same doors down. I had a chip on my shoulder that went back to feeling unpopular and resenting the kids who were popular, the feeling I had that I was as good as them, so why were they accepted and included, while I was excluded and cast out?

I looked down at the dog, but now, when I thought about the man who put him in the hole, I realized something.

In all the years that I was bullied, what seemed more unfair than anything else was the idea that the kids who held dominance over me—the bullies who belittled and mocked me because they were popular or had the support of their friends—were above me, and I was below them.

But that wasn't true. They were never above me. They were always below me, and for a lot of them and perhaps most of them, unless they saw the errors of their ways and changed, they would stay below me. I can't say that I was no longer angry at the man who put the dog in the hole, and I can't say that I felt sorry for him or that I pitied him, but now I saw the bully for who he was— someone who doesn't know what it feels like to be loved, and more to the point, someone who doesn't know how to love. The great Russian writer Leo Tolstoy once said, "Hell is the inability to love." That was exactly the hell the dog's tormentor was in.

Someone hurt him, so he hurt back, and hurt was probably all he would ever know. Somewhere along the line, something went wrong for him. I felt fairly sure that putting the dog in the pothole wasn't the first time he'd ever hurt an animal. He'd done it to get even, but he'd never know what "even" meant. I couldn't forgive him yet, but I could imagine how he felt, because I had something he lacked: I had empathy.

I had lifted the dog from the hole and restored him to the community of men. Whoever put him there was in a much deeper hole, and there was no way out of it, and it seemed doubtful that anyone would come looking for him or want to help him if they did. He was forever disconnected.

I'd talked to my therapist about how I have a strong reaction whenever I feel like I'm being treated unjustly or unfairly, or when something unjust or unfair happens to someone else. I am not exactly a crusader, in any public or political sense, but I could not abide injustice. I'd get upset, unable to let it go.

I found my cell phone and called Michelle.

"How'd it go?" she asked me. "How is he?"

"He's pretty tired still," I told her. "They think he's going to be okay. There might be complications."

"Where are you?"

"I'm on the road," I said. "I should be home by dinner time."

"Where's the puppy?"

"He's asleep on the floor beside me," I said.

It had occurred to me that I probably should have called her before deciding to bring the dog home, but knowing Michelle, I knew she wouldn't question the decision I'd made, and that she would have done the same thing. This puppy needed help, and we were capable of giving it to him. Plus, it could be said I risked my life for this little guy. That meant he was not only valuable to me, but to her, as well.

"From the sound of it, if I left him there, nobody would have adopted him anyway. After all we've been through, there's no way I was going to allow him to be euthanized."

"No," she said. "I can see that. So you're bringing him home?"

"At least until we can figure something else out," I said. "Do we know anybody who wants a dog?"

"I don't know," she said. "I'll be sure to have Kohi's crate ready with some towels, food, and water."

Deep down, I may have known that there was a new member of the family, but I wasn't willing to admit it yet.

The first hour of the drive home was uneventful. The dog kept looking up at me and I kept looking down at him. He was curled up in the passenger foot well, facing toward the back. Instead of tucking his head and snout toward his tail like you'd expect, he kept arching his head toward me, which looked incredibly uncomfortable, his head wedged between the cushion and the center console. Every time I put his head back where I thought it belonged, he'd wait for me to let go of his head and then return to the same position. It was like a game we played for the first hour to Kanab. I stopped to get my usual chocolate milk at a gas station, and then we proceeded north on 89. Thirty minutes later, we had our first problem. He'd been pretty still and quiet so far, but he suddenly began to squirm and started making whimpering, pleading sounds. I could see him trying to move, but he didn't have the strength to do what he wanted. I pulled off onto the gravel shoulder, walked around, and opened the door. I guessed he needed to relieve himself. I picked him up, which was shocking because he was still literally skin and bones. I was sure I was going to break him.

I carried him to where the shoulder ended, figuring he might feel more comfortable in the weeds. I placed him in a standing position on the ground. He looked like those nature videos you see on National Geographic or the Discovery Channel showing some newborn calf or elk taking their first steps, wobbly and hunched over. Possessing no motherly instincts, I just sort of hovered with

151

my hands on either side of him to provide support. He took a very awkward half step forward with his front paws to extend his body and urinated. I thought, *How 'bout that? I got it right.*

After he was done, he arched his back and extended his tail parallel to the ground, a position I recognized from my dog. For some reason, it seemed like peeing was one thing, but if he had to poop, a bit of privacy was in order, so I pulled back. I waited for something to happen, but things seemed stuck, the dog hovering uncomfortably in position. As I approached, he stumbled. I quickly grabbed him, and we avoided a fall. I managed to get him back where he needed to be, and again we waited. I felt ill prepared for dealing with something like this.

Just when I thought I could see some . . . progress . . . everything stopped again, and it was clear to both of us that something was amiss. He tried to walk, still in a hunched over position, precarious and unsteady.

I once again hovered above him, keeping my hands on either side of his ribs to catch him if he fell again, and I followed him around as he tried in vain to get things moving. I was on the verge of panic, thinking I might have to directly intervene, though how would I do that? I placed my fingers on either side of his rump and used a pinching motion to try to get the last of things moving. I was never one who could handle things like this gracefully, and I was literally gagging at being so close to the action. My heart also broke to watch this puppy struggle like this. Thankfully, after about twenty seconds, our combined efforts paid off. The proceedings came to conclusion and the pup finished what needed to be done. I was relieved, and so was the puppy, albeit in a different way.

An hour later, we repeated the previous episode, but the fact that his alimentary canal was again functioning was all good. The second time, he lost his balance and fell right over, smack into the ground without any attempt to brace or right himself. I felt immediately sad, and then livid about the situation—couldn't the poor dog catch a break? I ran over and helped him back up and then, once again resorting to my training as a Marine, I improvised and adapted, using a modified massage technique to get him started, but my nerves were beyond frazzled.

For someone who has been shot at and been lost in the Los Angeles mountains for more than twenty-four hours in a snow storm, you'd think I'd be tougher than this, but I was ready to crack. The emotional weight I had been carrying since Sunday was starting to take its toll. I was absolutely drained. I was on Highway 20, crossing west to I-15. When I reached I-15, I headed north. I had cell reception and called Michelle to give her an update on our progress. My voice told the story of my situation. She shared some encouraging words and let me know she would help out as soon as I got back. That moment could not come soon enough.

When I finally reached my driveway, I got out of the truck and had to lie flat on my back on the concrete, aching and exhausted. When Michelle picked up the dog and felt how emaciated and fragile he was, she was reduced to tears.

I wasn't reduced to tears, but the drive home had left me feeling beaten down and depressed. What bothered me so much was knowing that I was once again in the undeniable presence of the kind of abuse and cruelty I was so familiar with, but this wasn't a memory or an image—this was tangible and palpable, the dog a living survivor and victim of human cruelty and abuse, morbidly malnourished and damaged. He looked and smelled and felt like death. The truck had actually taken on a smell that was making me sick. I wasn't just physically tired. I was spiritually tired, exposed to a kind of soul-crushing poison that radiated from the poor animal and left me feeling down. I kept thinking, "You poor thing," and it's not hard to go from there to wondering about the kind of world we live in.

We kept Kohi and the puppy apart at first. Dr. Roundtree had suggested that before we put them together, we needed to have the puppy vaccinated and tested for infectious diseases. We brought the puppy to our vet in Salt Lake City, who gave him the standard protocol of shots and even gave the dog a full body X-ray, and after he had the film developed, he put it up on the light box for us to read. He pointed out something he found interesting: a half dozen distinct dots, smaller than BBs. When I asked him what they were, he said it was his opinion that somebody had shot the dog with a shotgun, and mostly, but not entirely, missed. If I ever had any doubts that we were doing the right thing, this moment erased them all.

When we finally introduced the two dogs, outdoors in the driveway where they wouldn't feel cramped, the puppy nipped at the older dog, even though I knew Kohi was only trying to be friendly, but it was heartening, all the same, to see the puppy still had a bit of fighting spirit in him. We separated them, and when we introduced them again, the same thing happened, but this time I let the puppy know, with a gentle but firm whap under the chin and a simple no, who was in charge. It was the last time we ever had a problem.

Within a week, the puppy was strong enough to walk and even run a little, and he'd gained weight. We kept close watch over him for convulsions or seizures, but he seemed fine, and as far as we could tell, his vision was 20/20, or whatever it was in dog terms. I could detect no signs of mental impairment or emotional damage, no head shyness, no lethargy. He did have an obsessive attachment to Michelle, which further solidified my belief that he had had bad experiences with men. I had the sense that after that single correction in the driveway, the new puppy was perfectly fine assuming the role of subordinate dog. It confirmed what I'd been thinking about the roles of dominance and subordination in Nature: that if animals had a drive to dominate and be the top wolf in the pack or the alpha stallion in the herd, they had a mutual or parallel need and drive to collaborate and cooperate and contribute to the cohesion and success of the group. He didn't care that he wasn't number one. He was just glad he had a number. His life had an order to it.

Oddly, mine seemed to have less. The euphoria and satisfaction of having rescued a dog that was nearly dead gave way to a sense of confusion and displacement. The night I got home from Page with the new addition, Michelle and I stayed up late into the night, as I filled her in on all the details I hadn't been able to give her. I'd been holding in a lot of emotions, and now that I was home with Michelle at my side, I could let them out.

Yet it didn't clear the air or settle anything. Finding the puppy had evoked an entire chain of memories and, in a way, disassembled an understanding I'd constructed about who I was and where I wanted to go with my life. Over the next year, as I spent more time with the puppy—who was growing into a strong, healthy, happy dog—I began to see things in new ways, but it was confusing because it was hard to remember the old ways, and then oddly, I realized that to do that, I needed to go back to where I came from—Cudahy, Wisconsin.

I decided a road trip was in order in January 2012. I stayed at my Uncle Greg's house. I didn't feel totally comfortable there, but it was safe enough. He'd kindly agreed to let me stay with him. I had with me a page of notes I'd made, things I wanted to talk to Sandra about. They weren't discussion points, but rather a black-and-white list of things that she refused to acknowledge.

Throughout the years, she'd been asking Michelle if she could explain to her why I had so many negative feelings toward her, and if nothing else, I didn't really appreciate my mother using my wife as a go-between. We'd had a fight about that very thing, the last time I'd seen her, nearly two years prior. It didn't seem possible, but somehow, she truly didn't understand where the dysfunction came from. When I started making notes about what I wanted to say to her, it took no more than ten minutes to fill the page with concrete examples. As the saying goes, you're entitled to your own opinions, but you're not entitled to your own facts. My notes were simply the facts.

I knew, of course, that she would argue about our separate interpretations of the facts, but I was not actually concerned about her interpretation of my notes. I just wanted her to confront the truth. What she did with it was up to her.

While in Cudahy, I called my mother from my cell one day and asked her if we could get together. She was extremely apprehensive, both because of how badly things went the last time I confronted her, albeit aggressively, and because she had always avoided confronting things head on.

We decided to meet on Sunday morning at 11:30. She suggested a restaurant, but I was pretty sure meeting at a restaurant wouldn't give us the privacy we needed. The last time we tried to talk, there was screaming, and there were tears, and if it happened again, I didn't want it to happen in a restaurant. Public parks were out for the same reason, but I wanted to talk to her somewhere open and neutral and, the more I thought about it, outdoors. I suggested a cemetery near her house, where we could talk without disturbing anybody.

I pulled into the cemetery at 11:29. Given her track record (after all, she'd missed half my wedding), I could only assume she'd be at least half an hour late, but to my surprise and amazement, she pulled in behind me in her Saturn station wagon, right on time—or, in fact, early.

She pulled up next to me. My mother wasn't in the best of shape physically, so rather than go for a walk, I got out of my car and took the passenger seat in hers.

"Michelle tells me you're apprehensive about meeting with me," I said.

"She wasn't supposed to tell you that," my mother replied.

"She's my wife," I said. "We don't keep secrets from each other."

"I'm just in a very vulnerable place right now," she said. "Mentally and emotionally. You have a history of saying things that hurt me."

A more accurate statement would have been to say *we* had a history of saying hurtful things to *each other*. I could certainly own my part of that.

"Yes, I do," I said. "That's true. That's a reasonable thing to say."

Because that was what we did, hurling accusations back and forth, each of us insisting that the other listen. I decided I was going to listen to what she said. If I didn't, I had no right to demand to be heard.

"I just don't know why you wanted to meet with me. Especially after how things went last time. You're just so negative toward me, and I don't know why."

"That's what's so frustrating," I said. "I keep trying to explain, and you never hear it. That's why I'm here. You act like you just can't understand why our relationship is so dysfunctional. I really didn't come here to throw stones or say anything to hurt you. I was hoping to provide some clarity and perspective. I don't see how we can ever fix this if we don't figure out what the problem is."

"Okay," she said, and she seemed relieved. "I just know you've spent your whole life holding grudges against the people you feel have wronged you. My own childhood was horrible, but I still had a relationship with my parents."

I thought of interrupting her to point out how dysfunctional her relationship with her own parents was, because I'd been thinking a lot about it, but I held my tongue because, again, I'd promised myself I would listen and not interrupt, even when I disagreed with what I was hearing. It was something I knew I needed to work on, in general; when I interact with people, I am often too quick to judge. There was nothing quick or sudden about my relationship with my mother, but the general rule still applied. We'd never understand each other if we couldn't get through to each other. For most of my life, I had concentrated on how to penetrate her defenses. I'd never thought much about how to lower my own protective armor and drop my shields, but I'd realized, lately, that it had to be a two-way street, so let it begin with me.

"Well, everybody's different," I said when she was finished. "No two people are going to react to the same situation the same way, and it doesn't necessarily mean one way is right and the other is wrong. I can't really say, 'You should have done what I did,' and you can't tell me I should have done what you did. We just do the best we can, right?"

I couldn't tell if my words were having any effect, but I was trying hard at least not to make things worse.

"It's not a competition to see which one of us had the worst childhood," I said. "Or who has the most right to complain about it. I was able to turn things around for myself in ways that you never could. But you're right. I hold grudges. We're both flawed. We're just not going to get anywhere if you expect me to be you and vice versa."

It occurred to me that this was probably the longest she'd ever listened to me without interrupting or refuting or contradicting what I was saying. This was a level of mutual courtesy I'd never experienced before with her. Calling it a mutual respect would signify that we'd taken a giant leap, when we were still taking tentative baby steps, but something was different. It was as if we agreed on what we held in common, which was a level of pain or emotional suffering, even though part of the pain we had caused each other. It was like two prizefighters at the end of a long fight, both bruised but both still standing, or two opposing soldiers at the end of a long war. It was time for the war to end.

"I'm sure Mark would have agreed with you about me holding grudges," I said. "He'd be justified to say he felt that way, so I suppose you are, too. It's just hard for me to let go when someone doesn't take responsibility for what they've done. There are two sides in every conflict and they won't get resolved unless both sides own up. Mark was frustrated with me, but he never communicated that. I mean, not as it grew. He just held it in until one day he exploded. Instead of telling me his perspective and working to understand mine, he just took it over the top. He never really tried to solve the problem. I think you and I do the same thing. That's why our relationship is so horrible. Or that's one reason, anyway. Do you remember when we went to family counseling, when I was sixteen?"

"Yes, I remember," she said. "That didn't work out."

"Maybe it didn't work for you," I said, "but I loved it. What I remember was going into it with an open mind, because I was really curious to see what might happen. And the guy didn't take sides. He just listened to both of us and gave us honest feedback, whether it was what we wanted to hear or not. He was very objective. I thought so. But it felt like you went in, hoping you'd find an ally who'd take your side against your out-of-control son. You didn't want to fix things. You wanted to be right. I don't think the point of family therapy is for one side to say, 'I give up—you win.'"

She seemed to agree with that, though she still didn't say anything. I explained to her how I'd been dealing with a lot of issues lately, depression and a general sense of pessimism, and physical back pains. I told her I'd been having problems at work, and problems making favorable impressions on people, and problems with anger and resentment and feeling the need to guard myself all the time. It all started at grade school, with the kids who tormented me, and then middle school, but also at home, with her. Finding our new dog had opened my eyes to a lot of things, including the need to make some changes in my life.

"Let me ask you," I said. "And this might sound strange, but . . . did you think it was a good idea for you and Mark to have kids? I mean, at the time, did you think you were ready?"

"I certainly did," she said.

"I know this is going to sound cold, but given the way things turned out, sometimes, I've just wished you hadn't," I said. "There's nothing you can do about it now, obviously, and don't get me wrong—I'm glad to be alive—but what I endured was just so destructive to me, as a person. There've been times when I thought it would have been better not to have me."

There was a long period of silence, but it wasn't an awkward silence. I wasn't waiting for the other shoe to drop or preparing a defense of what I'd said. I was just waiting for what I'd said to sink in. Finally, I thought maybe I needed to lighten the conversation.

"But not so much, lately," I said. "Michelle tells me you've been dating somebody. He's older?"

She nodded.

"Is he good for you?"

"For the most part, yes," she said. I was glad for her. She'd never had much luck with men. The words "for the most part" set off alarms, but I wasn't going to second guess her or warn her, because I didn't really know the situation.

There was another brief silence. I couldn't imagine that either one of us was feeling exactly comfortable, but we were there in the car together, paired forever by fate, or blood, or genes, or whatever you want to call it.

"Listen," I said finally. "I just wanted you to know something. I've been doing a lot of thinking lately, talking to Michelle and talking to a therapist, and thinking about how people who've been victims can turn around and victimize someone else. Or teach someone how to be a victim. And I wanted you to know that I realized something I never really thought about before. I was thinking about how you grew up. How Roland was diagnosed as schizophrenic, and Alice was, well, emotionally unsupportive, to say the least. I know you called it a 'chemical imbalance,' but that makes it sound sort of trivial or minor. And I'm sure it wasn't trivial or minor to you."

It was odd, I realized, because in a way, for the first time, I was able to put myself in her shoes, and walk a mile in them, and see things the way she saw them. At the same time, I felt like I'd walked a lot more than a mile and knew, in all the worst ways, what it was like for her, growing up, because she'd done to me what her parents did to her. She taught me what she'd been taught. How was she supposed to know more, or better? I mean, she could—we can all learn more than what our parents taught us, and become better people for it—but that wasn't her. She was too passive, too unable to take the initiative. Too unlikely to believe she was capable of changing. Or maybe she just hadn't been interested in learning, even though I'm sure she could see that things hadn't worked out for her.

"I know growing up on the North Side was hard. And I know that you were singled out, at Catholic school, for being unlike everybody else. By the nuns, and by some of the other students. I know how rough that was for you. You suffered in a lot of the same ways I suffered, at the hands of others. I'd never really considered how much of a victim you were, until recently, and I blamed you for things you couldn't help. I'm sure you didn't want to be a victim any more than I did, but I never gave you the benefit of the doubt."

I felt myself softening inside, and years of bitterness and resentment ever so slightly slipped away as we spoke. I could let go of it—not all of it and not all at once, because this wasn't going to be one of those dramatic final scenes in the movies where everything gets tied off neatly with a big bow in the ribbon—but even so, it was a turning point. We'd both been left at the bottom of a canyon. I was climbing out. She couldn't. Not yet, anyway.

"I'm not saying it's an excuse, and it doesn't make what I went through any less painful, but I understand why it happened. You taught me what your parents taught you. That's not necessarily a good thing, but that's how it works. That's why this is so dysfunctional."

She nodded again.

"I did a lot of things I regret," she said.

"But yet you still don't seem to comprehend why our relationship is so lousy," I said. "That is why I have created a list for you so you can see my issues with you in black and white. No more of this 'I just don't understand why he hates me so much' stuff." I handed her the list, which was just a typewritten piece of paper. She read it from start to finish without commenting along the way. I had no idea what she was thinking.

She finally spoke. "You always say I didn't try to protect you from Robin," she said. "I can't agree with that."

"Maybe you need to pretend otherwise, but you can't tell me you didn't know what was going on," I said. "Even my babysitter saw me nearly throw up one day, when Robin was coming to pick me up, and I was so scared it made me sick."

"You're right," my mother said. "I can't say I didn't know."

Now she was crying. It felt like some sort of veil had lifted from her eyes. Now she was seeing. I felt like I was witnessing an awakening. She seemed different. I could imagine some other mother and son, some other scene from some other movie, where the son would put his arm around his mother and say, "Don't cry, ma—I still love you," but that wasn't us. Not yet, anyway. We'd been in the car for about forty-five minutes, and so far we'd barely made eye contact. I thought we both deserved a lot of credit for not screaming and cursing each other out.

"I hope you can get the kind of help I've gotten," I said. "I know you didn't think that therapist we saw helped, but I think it would be good if you could sit down and talk to somebody who can help you be honest about things. Sometimes it's hard to look at stuff, but it's worth it. And I hope you can find happiness with this new guy you're seeing. I really do."

I stepped out of the car and realized there was no need to say "I'll see you later," because I couldn't say when that would be, but it would happen, someday, somewhere. Maybe the reason we had such a hard time talking about our relationship was that there was no way to do it without the pain coming back, reopening wounds that wouldn't heal, as we each reenacted our roles, fighting the same fight over and over again. That hadn't happened this time, but we needed to step back, and go to our corners, and spend some time thinking about what had just happened.

The air outside the car was cold and crisp, and I filled my lungs with it.

I decided that as long as I was in Wisconsin and confronting the demons of my past, I'd call Robin to see if she was willing to talk. She lived in Racine, about fifteen minutes away from where I was staying. I called her number and left a message on her answering machine, and I told her if she wanted to meet me, call back, but it wouldn't have disappointed me much if she hadn't. Two days later, she did. I agreed to meet her at her house. I arrived around 7:30 in the evening, and when she answered the door, no pleasantries were exchanged. I asked her where she wanted to talk. She led me to the living room, where she sat in her recliner with a quilt over her. I sat on the couch facing her. Unlike my mother, I didn't have any problem looking Robin in the eye. She returned my stare, but with a sense of weakness and pain. I could only imagine the personal trials she'd been dealing with since losing my father. In fact, she'd found him unconscious in the very room where we now spoke.

I opened by asking her if she remembered the night Michelle and I came over for dinner, and my father and I had had our falling out. She said she didn't remember anything about that night. The conversation deteriorated from there, so feeble an attempt at communicating that it's barely worth trying to reconstruct. She said she'd only agreed to meet me because she owed it to my father, and then she pointed to a picture of him on the wall. She admitted that in the years that I'd stayed with them, she'd been young and stupid, and that she'd never wanted me in her life because she'd married Mark, not me, and that she'd "f—ed up, but what the hell am I supposed to do about that now?"

That became the refrain, her answer to every question I had, whether it was applicable or not: "What do you want me to do about it now?" At one point, she even made her own suggestion. "What do you want me to do about it now—OD on a bunch of pills? Would that make things better?"

I held my tongue.

"I always felt stupid around you." Again, I thought of a dozen snappy comebacks, but I didn't need to go there. Seeing her sitting there, quilt on her lap, tears in her eyes . . . Life was punishing her. She was reaping what she had sowed. I did not envy her situation. In fact, it scared me.

And besides, I had really already gotten what I had come for. She was not sorry for her behavior that Monday night when Michelle and I had come over for dinner, or for the way she treated me as a kid. To her, it was simply an unfortunate situation, something that happened a long time ago, and as she said a dozen times, "So what do you want me to do about it now?"

If I felt sorry for her, it was the same way I felt sorry for the man who put the dog in the canyon, someone who was trapped in a hell of their own design and unable to climb out of it. Without my father, she was all alone, and that probably wasn't going to change. Nothing anybody could say would help—certainly nothing I had to say would end her suffering.

"Well, you won't have to worry about it," I said, rising from the couch. "I won't be contacting you again."

When I got back to Salt Lake City after visiting my mother, my dogs both greeted me with total exuberance. That may be what I like so much about dogs, the complete lack of guile or pretense. They are what they are, and when you catch them doing something they shouldn't, like sticking their head in the garbage can under the sink because they smell something interesting, they'll hang their heads and slink away in an admission of guilt.

By now, we'd had the puppy for more than a year and a half, and, of course, he had a name. We'd considered Shadow because he literally was Michelle's shadow for the first couple of months. Ultimately we named him Riley, as in the phrase "the life of Riley," which was the life we intended to give him. We looked up the origin of the word and learned it was most prominently featured in a radio show called *The Life of Riley*, but dated back to at least WWI and possibly to the Reilly clan in County Cavan, Ireland, a family so well off that they minted their own coins, known as O'Reilly's. The phrase means living a life of ease.

Riley toughed it out and got stronger day by day. He recovered his physical health (except for his brown teeth, which will never turn white) and his emotional health, as well—if he's carrying scars with him, they don't show. At first he was shy around people, but gradually recovered his playful instincts, chewing on toys and even, respectfully, initiating dog-on-dog roughhousing. In a sense, we gave him a chance to be a puppy again.

He didn't know how to play with humans, at first. When I tried to play with him, throwing a stick or a ball or trying to get him to "wrestle," he was initially confused and didn't know how to respond. Over time, as I brought him with me wherever I went, to work or hiking on weekends, he grew to trust me and he came to understand my intentions were playful.

If someone were to say to me that I saved Riley in the nick of time, I might agree. If someone were to say he came into my life, just in the nick of time, to save me, I would wholeheartedly agree. Before I found him, I felt beaten down, pessimistic, happy in my marriage but pessimistic about people, and tired of the constant struggle. When I thought of how long Riley must have struggled in that hole, I asked myself if I would have had the same will to live, and I'm not sure I would have.

What is so remarkable about Riley, and what I see every day that I'm with him, is his heart and his capacity for forgiveness. From the moment I saw him, my heart went out to him, and I wanted only to show him compassion and kindness, but in the act of giving compassion and kindness to him, I've exercised a kind of muscle in myself, and it has grown stronger. It's not the kind of muscle you can develop in a gym. You develop it by giving. Someone once said being angry at someone is like *you* drinking poison and expecting *them* to die—anger damages the vessel that contains it. Forgiveness flushes away the poison and leaves you healthier. Before I found Riley, I was full of anger, full of poisons, and holding it all in, carrying it with me wherever I went. He showed me the foolishness of that at a time when I truly needed to let go of the pain I was still carrying.

I'm still a work in progress, don't get me wrong, but I'm not lost in the winding canyons of the heart, looking for cairns to find my way back. I am actually finding my way forward. I look at Riley and think of the difference between humans and our animal counterparts—our higher intelligence has endowed us with long-term memories and a greater capacity to learn, but that comes with both a benefit and a cost. The cost is that we don't forget the things we should forget, or unlearn the things we should unlearn. We are easily shaped, in our formative years, by circumstances from which it can take us the rest of our lives to recover. But at any rate, I am no longer out for revenge, or perhaps I am insofar as the old saying goes, "living well is the best revenge."

It is now. I am exploring the San Rafael Swell in central Utah, a massive dome-shaped uplift of sandstone and limestone that pushed up forty to sixty million years ago, an area filled with canyons and mesas and buttes and valleys, but this time I'm not alone. I invited Michelle to join us, but she said she thought I needed a little time with the boys. I've left my ropes and climbing gear behind, because this is not a technical canyon. In my backpack, I have only water, Clif Bars, and dog treats.

Riley runs ahead of me, with Kohi right behind him, their noses to the ground and their tails wagging. Like me, they are excited because they want to know what's up around the corner, what's waiting for us. Life is an adventure for them, and for me, as well. At no time during the day does Riley shy away or flinch in the narrow canyons, and, in fact, he usually leads the way. He runs ahead, runs back to Kohi and me, exploring every dark nook and cranny. He is completely at ease. He is the living example of perseverance, resiliency, and the willingness to forgive, forget, and move on. In short, he's okay.

And in short, so am I.

CONCLUSION

When I began writing my story, I wondered how it would end. I had someone tell me that all stories need a happy ending with all of the loose ends tied up nice and neat. Well, from Riley's point of view, that's how he sees it. I don't know what darkness filled his life prior to me finding him. I don't know how he would have survived had I not pulled him out of that pothole. But I do know that June 20, 2010, was what I call his "re-birthday"—the day his previous life ended and his new, much happier one began. I feel a real sense of satisfaction knowing that I could do that for another creature. I look at that silly dog in a way I doubt I will ever look at another animal. I think he looks at his silly human the same way sometimes, too.

My story, on the other hand, hasn't quite played itself out yet. I have come a long way in the past couple of years. In that time I have had several teachers. Some of them professionals, one of them a woman who I see every morning when I wake up, and one of them a four-legged goofball who still says hello by licking me when I'm not looking, in spite of my protests. Each of them has played a role in helping me see things from a different perspective;

that is, a perspective that is not from within the confines of the fortress I built as a child—one of mistrust, cynicism, and fear.

The great irony for me and people like me is that we don't even know we are seeing the world from behind our fortresses. They are such a part of us that we just go through life seeing everyone first as a threat, then assessing the risk, and then finally deciding if they can be trusted. I never knew that perspective or that approach was causing people to feel uncomfortable around me, which of course contributed to the very behavior I came to expect from people. It was in many ways a self-fulfilling prophecy that reinforced my belief system about virtually everyone I met.

So is having this self-awareness enough? Am I all better now? I truly wish I was. I wish I could say that everything now makes sense. On a logical, unemotional level it does. I have spent the time talking it through with two people in particular who had the skills to pull back the curtain and help me see why I find myself bashing my way through the world. That realization was absolutely critical to beginning the healing process. After all, if you don't understand why things are going a certain way in your life, how can you begin making the necessary changes to rectify the problems you're having?

Finding safety in logic and understanding, I was hoping that once I had these answers I would be able to solve things in one swift motion. That's my style: get in there and get it done. And God knows I wanted this all to be done with. My depression, my back pain, my struggle with people . . . I just wanted it all to go away. But it didn't, and it hasn't.

Instead, I now realize that this is going to be a process. Someone explained it like this to me: the trauma you suffered was done on an emotional level. Logic is not going to solve it; you will need to solve it on an emotional level.

That was a real wakeup call. I'm practical enough to know that she was probably right, but I didn't want her to be. I don't know how to solve things, deeply personal things that involve my past. The fear and pain simply feel overwhelming. But that is what I must do. That is the journey before me. It's up to me to continue down this path and try to find contentment and peace in a world I don't trust. It's up to me to let go of the hate I have for the people who hurt me. Someone else told me that acid, i.e. hate, destroys the container it's held in. Truer words have never been spoken.

Riley serves as a daily reminder that all of this is possible. When I posted photos of him romping around with the family in a canyon on his Facebook page, a couple people made comments about causing him flashbacks by taking him there. What they didn't understand was that he was *not* in that same deep canyon I found him in. He was out in nature with his family, and these were places that needed to be explored.

This is the wisdom of our dogs. They acknowledge the past for what it is and don't carry it forward into their futures, unless people give them reason to. Sure, there are dogs that are fearful and aggressive from past abuse. And in Riley's case, he was still a puppy. The abuse had not taken place over years and years. I recognize that. But nevertheless, once someone came into Riley's life who proved worthy of trust, he went with it. He didn't carry the fear and mistrust of people with him the way we humans so often do.

And so I live each day, reminding myself how happy he is, how trusting he is. A slot canyon is not something to be feared or avoided any more than a car is something to be feared because you may have been in an accident. Life happens. It's what we make of it that really defines who we become. For my part, I am doing my best to undo years of neurological programming that said I cannot trust anyone, people are dangerous. It didn't happen overnight and it won't be resolved overnight. As I have been known to say, anything truly worth having is worth working for. And so my work continues.

My hope is that my story has some sort of lasting impact on your life. Our children are vulnerable—vulnerable to bullies who abuse them and vulnerable to the apathy of the adults in their lives. I hope the insights I have shared with you compel you to take action should you ever become aware of a child who is dealing with bullying, no matter what form it takes. Sometimes it will be from their peers, other times it will be from the adults in their lives. Regardless of the source, I ask that you step in on behalf of that child and do what's right. Had someone done that for me, I wonder how much damage could have been prevented, damage that causes me to struggle through things to this day.

In the very beginning of this book, I wrote the definition of character as I once heard it. For a child's sake, I beg you, please do what's right, *especially* if nobody is watching.

Thank you!

Page Arizona Animal Hospital
Angel Fund

The folks at Page Animal Hospital picked up where I left off. I got Riley out of the canyon, but they brought him back into this world. He would not be here with his family today if it had not been for the skill and kindness of the entire staff!

If you would like to make a donation on Riley's behalf to their Angel Fund, which is used to save injured animals who have no home, I would be extraordinarily grateful. They are constantly dealing with injured animals from the surrounding area, so any assistance they can receive will be dearly appreciated.

My heartfelt thanks go out to Dr. Roundtree and his incredible staff!

RESOURCES

We turned to these websites and articles to help us write the book and we highly recommend visiting them if you're interested in learning more about any of the topics discussed.

Cyberbullying Research Center
"Summary of our cyberbullying research from 2004–2010"
http://www.cyberbullying.us/research.php

Harford County Examiner
"From cyber bullying to sexting: What on your kids' cell?" by Richard Webster
http://www.examiner.com/article/from-cyber-bullying-to-sexting-stats-and-videos-what-s-on-your-kids-cell

i-SAFE.org
"Cyber Bullying: Statistics and Tips"
http://www.isafe.org/outreach/media/media_cyber_bullying

Make Beats, Not Beat Downs
http://www.makebeatsnotbeatdowns.org.olweua.org

National Crime Prevention Council
"Cyberbullying"
http://www.ncpc.org/cyberbullying

Riley's Official Facebook Page
https://www.facebook.com/canyonpuppy

RILEY'S STORY FEATURED ON THE WEB

In the days and weeks after Riley was rescued from the canyon, both local and national media picked up on the story. Here is a partial list of some of the media coverage Riley and Zak received.

KSL Salt Lake "Man Documents Daring Rescue of Puppy from Slot Canyon"
6/30/2010
http://www.ksl.com/index.php?nid=148&sid=11386233
This was the story that broke in Salt Lake City shortly after Riley was rescued.

The Today Show "Ace in the Hole"
7/2/2010
http://www.today.com/id/38054231/ns/today-today_pets/t/ace-hole-he-rescued-dog-trapped-canyon/#.UeRS521N-t9
Zak, Michelle, and Riley are interviewed by Meredith Vieira from their home in Salt Lake City. Riley was still recovering and basically slept through the interview.

Inside Edition "Abandoned Puppy Rescued in a Canyon"
7/7/2010
http://www.insideedition.com/headlines/880-abandoned-puppy-rescued-in-a-canyon
A camera crew from *Inside Edition* followed Riley and Zak around for a day to include a visit to the vet.

The Ellen DeGeneres Show
9/21/2010
http://www.youtube.com/watch?v=psQozLDnx7Q
Ellen flew Riley, Zak, and Michelle out to her studios to be guests on her show. She very generously gave Riley and his brother Kohi Halo dog food for life! She also provided Michelle and Zak with some extremely generous gifts!

Riley's Facebook page
https://www.facebook.com/canyonpuppy
With all of the media attention the story received we decided to create this page to communicate with all of the people who wanted to learn what happened to the puppy.

YouTube: Riley's Rescuing Video
Posted: 11/21/2013
https://www.youtube.com/watch?v=4KE6xmuqum0
This is the video I shot when I found and rescued an abandoned puppy in a slot canyon.